# THE CINEMA OF FRANÇOIS TRUFFAUT
by Graham Petrie

Above: Truffaut with Jean-Pierre
Cargol in *L'ENFANT SAUVAGE*

In the same series,
produced by THE TANTIVY PRESS
and edited by Peter Cowie:

# The Cinema of François Truffaut

by
GRAHAM PETRIE

THE INTERNATIONAL FILM GUIDE SERIES

A. S. BARNES & CO., NEW YORK

A. ZWEMMER LIMITED, LONDON

# Acknowledgements

I WOULD LIKE to thank Mr. Brian Linehan of the Janus Film Library (Canada) and M. André Pépin of Art-Films (Montreal) for their kind assistance in helping me to re-see some of the films discussed in this book. I am indebted also to Mr. Linehan, Mr. Normand F. Lareau (Stills from Foreign Films, New York), Les Films du Carrosse (Paris), United Artists (Toronto), Universal (London), Astor Pictures (New York), Janus Films (New York), Zenith International (New York), Gala Films (London), and Mr. Peter Cowie for their loan of stills, to Miss Helen Scott for providing valuable information about Truffaut's career, and to M. Truffaut himself for his encouragement and his allowing me to see the scenario for his recent film *L'Enfant Sauvage*.

### COVER STILLS

Front: Catherine Deneuve and Jean-Paul Belmondo in *La Sirène du Mississipi* (Courtesy of Les Artistes Associés, Paris). Back: Truffaut directing Julie Christie in *Fahrenheit 451* (Courtesy of Universal, London).

FIRST PUBLISHED 1970
*Copyright* © 1970 by Graham Petrie
Library of Congress Catalogue Card Number: 71-106791
SBN 498 07649 0 (U.S.A.)
SBN 302 02054 3 (U.K.)
*Printed in the United States of America*

# Contents

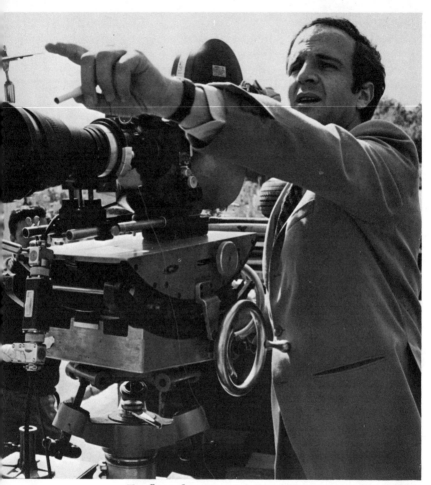

*Truffaut directing* LA MARIEE ETAIT EN NOIR

# Introduction

THE STRUCTURE OF THIS BOOK is an attempt to combine two of the main tendencies of traditional film criticism to date: the general theoretical work, and the study in depth of an individual director. The former normally proceeds by assembling examples taken from the whole range of film history, sometimes from very rare and inaccessible works, and the result may often be too rich or too diffuse: the reader is left with a strong sense of the potential and variety of cinematic resources, but with very little clear idea of how or why any particular film or the *oeuvre* of any particular director made the impact on him that it did. The latter is generally a sub-species of literary criticism, concentrating on themes, plot and characters to the exclusion of almost everything else, with the aim of coming to some sort of value judgement about the director's stature and his place in film history.

A newer and currently very fashionable approach to film (at least in North America) attempts to use film as a tool by which to understand better the contemporary environment, to study inter-personal relationships, social and political structures, and so on. The operative word here is "use;" this kind of critic is not interested in a film as a work of art, making its impact on the viewer because of its qualities *as* art, and for his purposes a bad film is just as useful as a good one—often more useful, for it will reveal underlying social and moral assumptions more starkly and crudely, untouched and unshaped by a personal or eccentric sensibility. This approach can be very illuminating, and I have clearly myself been influenced by it, but it is also very limiting and dangerous. Contempt for the artistic shaping of a film and its existence as part of an individual artist's developing expression of himself and the way he views the world can lead to grotesque distortions and falsifications of the film itself. The critic then tends either to come to the film determined to find one particular element in it, and naturally triumphantly doing so, or to isolate one perfectly valid facet and make this stand for the whole, twisting and misrepresenting the film to make it fit the pattern he has chosen. The result is that this type of criticism misleads as much as it illuminates, and the arrogance of refusing to respond to or to recognise the *whole* of the creative experience is more an impoverishment than an enrichment.

My own method is a synthesis of the first two, with an infusion of what I find of value in the third. I am interested in how and why one particularly gifted director uses the artistic means at his disposal—camera, editing, music, dialogue, sound effects, silence, colours, settings, objects, gestures, faces, actors, fictional characters and events—and how and why what he does with these affects us, the viewers of the films. The pattern of the book is that Chapter One deals mainly with camera and editing, Chapter Two with places, objects and settings as clues to, or conditioning elements of human behaviour, and Chapter Three with music, sound effects and dialogue. Between them these should set up a context in which the more traditional fourth chapter, dealing with characters and themes, becomes almost self-explanatory—for these elements cannot exist independently of the means by which they are created. For those readers who are frustrated by the constant jumping about from film to film in the body of the book, Chapter Five provides some comments on what is, at the date of writing, Truffaut's latest film.

This book contains little factual or biographical information, for Truffaut seems to wish to keep his private life his own affair. The most relevant facts are as follows: he was born in Paris on February 6, 1932 and had a childhood very similar to that of the hero of the semi-autobiographical *Les 400 Coups*

(*Les Quatre Cents Coups*), including a spell in a reformatory and working in a factory at the age of fifteen. His already avid interest in the cinema brought him to the attention of André Bazin, editor of *Cahiers du Cinéma,* and he quickly became known as one of the most outspoken young critics in the country. He did his military service in the army and, like the Antoine Doinel of *Baisers Volés,* deserted and spent time in various prisons as a result.* He then resumed his career as a film critic, made a 16mm short film, *Une Visite,* in 1955, worked as assistant to Roberto Rossellini in 1956, though none of the finished products have yet been shown, and in 1958 produced his first important work, *Les Mistons. Histoire d'Eau,* made with Jean-Luc Godard, followed in 1959, and his first feature *Les 400 Coups,* made on a relatively small budget, won the prize for best direction at Cannes in 1959 and the American Film Critics' award for best foreign film of that year, thus establishing both Truffaut and the emerging *Nouvelle Vague* on a firm basis. In 1960 he was one of the signers of the "Manifeste des 121," an appeal to soldiers in the French army to desert rather than fight in the Algerian War which was initiated by Jean-Paul Sartre and signed by 121 intellectuals. The very real danger of reprisals against him and the possible end of his film career was averted only by the conclusion of the Algerian War and the resulting amnesty. A steady stream of films has followed since then, most of them produced by his own company, Les Films du Carrosse (named after Renoir's *Le Carrosse d'Or*), and he has kept firm control over each aspect of them. He is married and has two daughters.

* * *

*According to sources close to Truffaut, the recent claim[9] that he joined and deserted from the French Foreign Legion has no basis in fact.

The comparison between what I call "open" and "closed" cinema which is made in the first chapter of the book is not intended in any way as a value judgement and does not imply that I think Truffaut's way of making films is intrinsically better than that of Godard, Bergman or Bresson. The comparison is itself valid only to a certain extent (though sufficiently so, I think, to make the point I wish to); looked at from another viewpoint or in another context, these film-makers can all, in their own ways, open up experience for us, and Godard in particular, especially in *A Bout de Souffle, Bande à Part* and *Pierrot le Fou,* has much more in common with Truffaut than I suggest.

*Tribute to Renoir: a shot from the opening of JULES ET JIM re-creates a scene from UNE PARTIE DE CAMPAGNE*

# 1. A Cinema of Discovery

A FILM-MAKER LIKE BRESSON, Godard or Antonioni creates in each of his films a consistent visual pattern which imposes itself and is recognisable whatever the ostensible subject-matter of the work. The visual world is filtered back to the viewer through other eyes, other sensibilities; the audience is forced for 90 or 120 minutes to see the world as Bresson or Antonioni sees it. The advantage of this method is that, if the director is sensitive or forceful enough, he can bring about a drastic re-organisation of accepted visual habits: the focus may be narrow, even distorted, but we quite literally *see* the world around us in a different way as a result of watching *The Red Desert, Pierrot le Fou* or *Au Hasard Balthazar*. We are forced to pay attention to aspects of our visual environment which are normally taken for granted, overlooked or ignored; if we respond positively to the film, we emerge with a new means of interpreting and shaping our daily experience. This re-shaping is primarily an aesthetic one; it is closely tied in to our reaction to the director's handling of cinematic structure, rhythm, movement, composition, editing, the use of landscape and setting. If we refuse to respond on the aesthetic level, then the film becomes meaningless to us: if we reject Godard's visual style, we reject with it his vision of the world, for the two are inseparable. It is no coincidence that it is film-makers of this type who rouse the most passionate controversy, the most heated defence and the most vicious attacks. It is impossible to remain totally indifferent towards them, and it is equally impossible to say something like: "I accept what he's saying, but I hate the way he says it."

The style of a director like Renoir or Truffaut does not present the same kind of immediate barrier to the viewer, yet at the same time it does not offer the kind of secure guideline that Antonioni's style does. Critics know where they stand with Antonioni; they know what they are expected to say and they say it—hence the proliferation of articles and books on Godard, Antonioni and Bergman (who imposes a "closed" moral or intellectual structure on his films, denying the viewer a glimpse of an alternative world as long as the films last—in its way equivalent to the visual selectivity of the other directors.) Truffaut and Renoir, however, are less concerned with moulding every aspect of their subject-matter to suit their own stylistic patterns; they have much more respect for the integrity of the material and of their characters, and they prefer to evolve a visual style which takes its impetus from what the subject requires rather than from what they intend to make out of it. The result is a more open kind of film-making, where the viewer is encouraged to make his own discoveries rather than being asked to accept or reject a particular interpretation of reality. The sensitive viewer of a Truffaut film will find himself making constant and subtle re-adjustments of his standard assumptions and preconceptions; he will emerge with a new awareness of the incongruous rhythms of life, of the inextricable mingling of beauty and sadness in everyday experience, but he will feel that he has discovered these for himself. Exactly because he *does* feel this, however, he may give the film-maker less credit than he deserves for the subtlety and intelligence with which he has brought about these re-adjustments. The style may seem so unobtrusive or "natural," the people so real, the behaviour so spontaneous, the final response so instinctive, that the viewer may feel less that he has been brought *to* this new stage of sensitivity than that Truffaut has merely brought it *out of* him. Though this may be partially correct, and it is a major element of Truffaut's genius that he is able to re-awaken in us the capacities for joy and tenderness which contemporary life forces us ruthlessly to submerge, it is far from the whole story.

＊　　＊　　＊

*Jules et Jim* is the film of Truffaut's in which the viewer is most likely to be conscious of visual style, though he will rarely feel that the style in itself imposes a certain set of responses on him, as it would in a film by Godard. At the end of the film we feel that the assessment we have come to of the characters and their behaviour is our own; it is only after a certain amount of later introspection that we may realise that we have come to tolerate, understand and sympathise with behaviour which most people would consider selfish, self-indulgent or even grotesque if encountered in ordinary life. Our responses then *have* been shaped and formed in the course of watching the film, yet there is *also* a genuine freedom left to us at the end: we are at liberty to refuse to extend this tolerance towards the characters if we wish to. If we make this decision, it does not necessarily imply a failure of Truffaut's visual style (whereas a refusal to sympathise with Giuliana in *The Red Desert* indicates stylistic failure on Antonioni's part); it means simply that at the end of a Truffaut film, the ultimate moral decisions are still our own. We have, however, gained a new flexibility, a new perspective, from which to make these decisions.

The most characteristic stylistic feature of *Jules et Jim* is the love of the film medium which pervades every foot of it. Truffaut conducts an intoxicating love affair with the cinema, determined apparently to exploit every visual resource at his disposal, yet the result and purpose are much more than mere stylistic virtuosity. The vitality and restlessness of the camera style reflect the nature of the characters and themselves impose a thematic structure on the film: the style subtly changes, slackens and slows down as the characters alter in the course of the film and different implications begin to be drawn from their behaviour. The film as a whole is full of movement and energy, but the type of movement involved varies, according to the circumstances, between that of the camera, that of the characters, and that created by cutting. At the beginning of the film, there is a need to suspend the audience's moral judgement on the apparently shiftless, amoral characters; this is achieved by involving the viewer emotionally through the pace and speed of events, forcing him to identify rhythmically with the characters before he can begin even to try to understand them. In the course of the film almost every possible visual device is employed: constant panning and tracking shots, hand-held camera, helicopter shots, crane shots, zooms, freeze-frames, superimpositions, masking, irises, while the editing technique varies from a series of very short shots moving rapidly about in time and space to several very long sequences filmed without a cut. Every device, however, is used for a specific purpose and contributes to creating the mood or the themes of the film. Truffaut uses the camera as a probe to uncover characters, setting and relationships in the course of the film; there is a sense of continuous revelation, of discovery, of fluidity, rather than of something set out and planned in advance. It is this kind of "openness" which is Truffaut's greatest stylistic contribution to the modern cinema.

The credits are given over a series of quickly edited shots of situations (some, though by no means all of them re-appearing later in the film) in which Jules, Jim, Sabine and Albert are by turns involved (Catherine does not appear in this section). These catapult us immediately into a sense of a particular time and place, a world of incessant activity, while the brash, brazen music accompanying the visuals begins already to exhilarate and excite. The pace is kept up in the introductory scenes which follow, in the breathless outpouring of words by the narrator, and in the series of shots of Jules and Jim where the period clothing, the comic or ridiculous activities, and the sense of friendship and companionship all combine to enlist our sympathy towards them. Most of these scenes are essentially static, the sense of pace and constant movement being supplied by the music, the continuity of the narrator's voice, the quick cutting within and between scenes, and a few sweeping pans joining one character to another. Then comes the introduction of Thérèse and her brief relationship with Jules; there is no let-up

*One of our first glimpses of Jim (Henri Serre—at left) and Jules (Oskar Werner)*

*Thérèse (Marie Dubois) does her "steamboat" trick for Jules*

in pace, the sense of comedy, of movement and vitality remain, but now the camera begins to create mood and atmosphere in such shots as the 360° pan which follows Thérèse round Jules's room as she does her "steamboat" trick with a cigarette. Even the potentially sad break-up of the affair and her desertion of Jules are turned to comedy by the camera (and the music): Jules and Jim argue about Shakespeare in a café while the bored Thérèse proceeds to attract the attention of a thoroughly unappealing little man; tracking shots follow her to the telephone and out of the door with him, as Jules and Jim are forgotten;

*Jim, Catherine and Jules at their seaside house*

then a whip-pan brings us back to the startled Jules. The constant movement of the camera, the buoyant music, the repetition of Thérèse's standard seduction technique with her cigarette, the comments of the narrator on Jim's attempt to buy the table on which Jules had chalked a picture of a German girl friend (the owner sold tables only by the dozen) all help to establish the desertion as part of the chaos of everyday existence rather than as something of lasting importance.

By this stage the audience is ready to believe almost anything, however unconventional or apparently ridiculous, about these two men. So we accept that they would rush off to the Adriatic after seeing a photograph of a Greek statue which had impressed them. The discovery of Catherine follows, and a relationship between the three builds up that is conveyed almost entirely through physical movement, a movement in which the camera joins, tracking back before them in their race across the bridge, then unashamedly abandoning neutrality to accompany and support Catherine, following them as they cycle through the countryside, wander through forests and tussle on beaches. At the same time the submerged tensions in the relationship are conveyed through physical separation: Catherine is often shown spatially detached from the two men, either in the famous triangle shot as the three look out of separate windows of their seaside house, or cycling slightly apart from them, or sitting on the beach as waves (Catherine's natural element is water) overwhelm her admirers, or sitting conspicuously away from the table as Jules and Jim play dominoes. The crucial scene that brings these tensions to the surface—Catherine's jumping into the Seine—is observed by a static camera; the movement, negative in its implications, is conveyed entirely through cutting.

From this point on the style of the film begins to change, the mindless exuberance of the characters gives way to a dawning recognition of the inevitability of responsibility and commitment. The film becomes an investigation of a series of hopeless relationships, attempts to avoid or compromise with the realities of possessiveness and jealousy. As the emotions become steadily more muted, so too does the camera settle down, except to join in moments of recaptured happiness (panning round the group at the chalet as they play their "village idiot" game, or following Jim and Sabine as they roll down the hillside) or to convey the new atmosphere of yearning and searching through helicopter shots which begin with Jim's visiting war cemeteries, sweep back and forth over the chalet, and later seem to plunge the viewer from a hilltop down into a valley as the "promised land" the characters long for recedes. The camera is still often in movement, but in a more sustained, coherent manner (following Jim and Catherine endlessly on their long walk through the countryside at night), and there are many more long-held static shots (e.g. when Jim tells his story about the soldier and his impossible love). In general, in the second half of the film, shots are held longer, the cutting is less deliberately obtrusive and disorienting, the mood quieter. The pace of the film thus alters to take account of an increasingly complex and painful situation (even the cycling shots now seem less exuberant), though the stylistic process comes full circle in the closing scenes. Catherine's death plunge is shot in a series of swift cuts between long-shots of the car crossing the bridge, medium-shots of Jules watching, and close-ups of Catherine smiling and of Jim seen through the windscreen. The cremation is filmed in a sequence of unsettling dissolves as the bodies go through the process of irrevocable destruction, and the last shot has the camera pan to follow Jules as he walks away, then hold still as the music of Catherine's song makes the final comment. The rhythm of the film, while it constantly reflects the reality of the characters' experience, is also continually carrying out a process of re-educating the viewer's sensibilities, inducing in him, through a series of unexpected and disconcerting stimuli, a new kind of emotional flexibility.

Throughout *Jules et Jim* the camera, by restlessly following the characters, forces the viewer to identify and associate himself with them. This is particularly true of close-ups, which bring the audience into inescapable identification with the figures on the screen—once again, whether we consciously *wish* this identification or not. When Catherine quarrels with Jim one night in the chalet and returns to the rejected Jules for comfort, the audience may be inclined to dislike her apparent exploitation of him, or to despise him for accepting it. But our intimate association with their faces as they hug each other, Catherine's streaked with tears as she tries to smile and convince Jules and herself that this time things will work out for them, Jules's sad and resigned as he accepts responsibility for comforting her yet clearly knows that the reconciliation is fragile and absurd—this intimacy inevitably precludes any application of conventional moral standards to the situation.

*The reconciliation between Catherine and Jules*

Throughout the film the camera is constantly exploring the characters, their faces, bodies, movements, and also the relationship between them and their environment. On the Greek island the camera searches, probes among the statues, hesitates, moves back and forwards from one to the other, until it finds the right one and triumphantly circles round it. When Catherine first appears the camera zooms in on her face in a series of quick shots from all angles, recalling the discovery of the statue, and her face is later explored, captured for a moment, then released in a series of freeze-frame close-ups—a perfect summation of her elusive beauty which the men too will try to capture and pin down. Freeze-frames also catch the uncertainty and awkwardness of the reunion between Jules and Jim after the War—nothing has changed, and yet everything has. Masking shots and irises isolate the characters at moments of emotional decisiveness—as Jules and Catherine are closed off together on the screen at the end of the party where they first meet. In the scene where Catherine is burning old love letters and her night-dress catches fire, a series of quick cuts and then an unsteady pan up to her frightened face capture the fear and anxiety of the moment. At the sea-shore the camera searches for relics with the characters—we see only their feet and hands and hear their voices. At the chalet when Jim and Catherine are standing outside talking about their new-found love and Jim asks what will happen to Jules, the camera moves hesitantly and awkwardly to search out and find Jules listening at the window above. In all these instances the camera itself becomes creative; it seems to be seeking out and establishing connections and relationships, and there is the sense of a film constantly in the process of discovery. The whole creative function of the camera is perhaps best summed up at the end of Catherine's song in the chalet where, with the word *"enlacés"* ("embracing," though the word can also mean "entwined" or "interwoven"), the

*"Tous les [quatres] enlacés": Catherine, Albert (Boris Bassiak), Jim, and Jules*

camera pans to join Albert, Catherine, Jules and Jim, then dissolves to the temporary "unity" of the cycling expedition. Throughout the film camera style, rhythm, editing and optical devices (the only "useless" one being the superimposition of Catherine's face on a helicopter shot of the landscape round the chalet as she reads a letter to Jim) all combine to create a sense of constant change, discovery, experiment, searching, revelation, restlessness, and final satiation. Style, theme, characters and the response of the audience blend into a unity that is characterised by fluidity and flexibility, an openness to the mystery and unpredictability of human experience.

❋   ❋   ❋

*Tirez sur le Pianiste (Shoot the Pianist/Shoot the Piano Player)*
is a gangster story that refuses to behave like a gangster story,
a love story that refuses to behave like a love story, a film that
refuses to conform to our assumptions about what a film can
and should do. Its unsettling and disorienting quality, however,
comes less from unusual or experimental camera techniques
than from bizarre and unexpected juxtapositions of mood, setting and action, from constant and sudden alternations between
farce and tragedy, and from the nature and behaviour of the
characters involved. The tone is established in the opening sequence, which presents us with the totally unexplained situation of a man fleeing from unseen pursuers (represented only
by the sound and headlights of their car). We are forced into
automatic identification with him, partly by his situation, and
partly through repeated close-ups of his anxious, hunted face.
While we are busy on the intellectual level trying to work out
the mystery of the situation, we are further unsettled visually
by the circumstances of the filming: normally a night scene of
this kind, even if shot (like this one) in real streets, would be
artificially lit in such a way that we could follow the characters
clearly. Here, however, only available light is used, with the
result that Chico (the man being chased) moves abruptly and
disconcertingly from the full glare of a street lamp into complete darkness, then back into half-light again, and into shots
of this kind are intercut jarring flashes of the headlights of the
pursuing car. A sudden long-shot abruptly distances us from
Chico: we see him stumble and hurtle, in almost comic fashion,
into a lamp-post; laughter at the awkwardness of his fall is
stifled by our realisation that he seems to be hurt. He lies there
moaning, we hear footsteps, we see someone bend over him
ominously and slap his face. The newcomer helps him up, we
expect him to be an enemy and are prepared for violence, but
Chico simply brushes himself off, thanks him, and the two

walk off together like old friends. They begin a conversation which quickly takes a very personal turn and Chico's helper takes the opportunity to tell a perfect stranger details of his private life which he could tell no one else. He talks about love, sex, the disillusionments and compensations of marriage as they walk on through patches of light and darkness, his voice competing with the sound of their footsteps and the roar of traffic. They stop at a corner and say goodbye, the other leaves, Chico looks round and abruptly begins to run again—we are suddenly reminded that the danger to him was neither imaginary nor forgotten.

Almost every feature of this sequence is designed to disorient the audience: Raoul Coutard's deliberately rough camera style, the lighting (or lack of it), the total absence of background music that might help the audience to develop an appropriate emotional response, and especially the confusion as to whether and when we should experience fear, relief or laughter, and to what extent we are intended to identify with the characters. This uncertainty continues throughout the film: in the sequence that follows in the bar where Charlie works, the violence of the gangsters' pursuit of Chico and Charlie's intervention to foil them is followed by the inanity of the waiter's ridiculous song —ridiculous both in its nonsense words and the jerky, puppet-like movements of the singer (yet the words, emphasising the incongruity of sexual relationships, relate to a major theme of the film). Other scenes inside the bar have a strange, unsettling quality—Chico seizes, dances with and propositions the barman's mistress all within the space of a couple of minutes; Charlie's prostitute girl friend is seen conducting a strange dance with a young man in which she lures him to her then pushes him contemptuously away, finally provoking him to violence; we are given brief glimpses of background conversations about sex and of tentative sexual advances between people

The fight sequence in
TIREZ SUR LE
PIANISTE. From left to
right, Charlie (Charles
Aznavour) intervenes when
the barman (Serge Davri)
threatens Lena (Marie
Dubois); is in turn at-
tacked; seizes a carving
knife; and, after a brief
reconciliation outside, de-
fends himself desperately...

25

dancing. All these scenes are thematically viable, but the way in which they are presented causes us to start questioning actions and responses we had previously taken for granted.

The film is full of incidents where serious actions are shot in a comic way: Charlie is abducted by having a quite monstrous gun pointed at his nose in the middle of the street and Lena is bustled into the gangsters' car while passers-by look calmly on (this scene may well have been shot with a hidden camera); once in the car, however, captors and captured get on well together, joke and reminisce about their childhood. This approach is crystallised in the scene of the killing of the barman, which begins with the quarrel between Lena and the barman, from which Charlie attempts to remain detached, but which reaches a pitch of virulence that forces him to intervene. A ridiculous yet potentially dangerous duel of telephone receiver against carving knife follows, the absurdity of it being heightened by wildly over-emphatic music; Charlie chases his opponent outside but throws down his knife and attempts reconciliation; there is a moment of relief and exhaustion, till the apparently friendly gesture by the barman of putting his arm round Charlie's shoulder turns into attempted murder as he tries to choke him. This scene is shot in dispassionate close-up as the expressionless barman talks (as does every character in the film once given the opportunity) of his life-history and the misery of his sex-life, while Charlie gasps helplessly for breath beside him. Then comes the struggle for possession of the knife and the ambiguous stabbing, in which Charlie seems to use rather more force that he later claims he did or intended to. In this scene, as almost everywhere else in the film, camera virtuosity is secondary to abrupt changes of mood established by cutting or juxtaposition within the frame, together with brusque transitions in place and action. The two most pervasive stylistic features—the hand-held camera and the relentless use of available light, which often leaves the screen in near-complete darkness (elements which are combined in the long sequence of Charlie's arrival at the farm and walk up the hillside with his brother Richard)—create a deliberate visual roughness, a lack of normal technical polish, that by breaking down our stylistic preconceptions about film, enable us to accept more readily this world where farce, sadness, violence, death and laughter clash and coincide. We are not, of course, being shown a new world; we are simply seeing our own world, as though for the first time, with unprecedented spontaneity, freshness and vitality. By breaking down our accepted notions of cause and effect, by destroying our normal expectations and assumptions about pattern and order and neat categorisation of experience, Truffaut has given us a means of apprehending the real world around us more intelligently and perceptively, for it is the real world he has shown us.

There are some occasions in *Tirez sur le Pianiste*, particularly in the love scenes, where the camera is allowed to take on the kind of creative function characteristic of *Jules and Jim*. In the early scene between Charlie and Clarisse (the prostitute) a mood of purely sensuous and physical pleasure predominates, an atmosphere of almost routine yet still enjoyable behaviour. There is something ritualistic about the spatial detachment and separation of the lovers: Charlie lies in bed watching Clarisse undress and, despite (or perhaps because of) their obvious long familiarity with each other, she feels the need to titillate and stimulate him with a kind of strip-tease performance, hiding behind a screen and displaying piece by piece each segment of her seductive black underwear. (Characteristically for this film, having waved her black panties at him, she proceeds to emerge unexpectedly wearing her slip.) The sense of voyeurism is heightened by the way in which the camera pans to follow her, as though through Charlie's eyes, as she moves about the room. Finally she emerges nude (the uncut version of the film pokes fun at both the censor and the voyeuristic instincts of the audience by including a shot in which she is allowed to expose her breasts and Charlie immediately covers them with a sheet, telling her that the censor wouldn't approve). With an expression of comical lust on his face Charlie proceeds to wind up his alarm clock, put out the light and dive under the sheets with her, to the accompaniment of muffled squeals on her part. The effect of the whole scene is external, detached; there is a sense of welcome physical enjoyment but little or no emotional commitment—the impression of a performance or a routine (heightened by brief shots of Charlie's metronome and by the reference to the censor) is strong.

*Charlie and Clarisse (Michèle Mercier)*

The two flashback love scenes between Charlie and his wife have a quality of tension and false reconciliation. In the quarrel scene, as Theresa tries to tell him how much he has changed, the camera pans to and fro angrily with Charlie, then a close-up of his face turns out disconcertingly to be a mirror-shot, the camera moves to bring her "real" presence into frame while he remains a reflection, finally both become briefly "real" as reconciliation is reached and a gentle pan accompanies them as they relax on to the bed. The fragility and misunderstandings of the relationship are conveyed vividly through the camera movements and the framing. In the later scene where Theresa confesses her affair with the impresario Schmeel the camera follows her as she wanders round the room desperately trying to explain, close-ups of her face against a blank white background emphasise her isolation, and a close-up catches Charlie's indecision as he tells himself to go to her and help her but inevitably makes the wrong decision and leaves.

In contrast to the scenes with Clarisse and Theresa, the one physical and detached, the camera content merely to observe, the other emotional and involving as the camera forces us into proximity with the characters, the love scene with Lena is both remote and immediate, serene and unsettling. After the flashback to Charlie's earlier career the camera returns to the poster of him as Edouard Saroyan the pianist on Lena's bedroom wall, then pans slowly round the room taking in furniture, ornaments, discarded clothing; a close-up of Lena and Charlie kissing is superimposed on this, then vanishes as the shot ends on the two of them in bed. Lena is talking to him, he is passive, perhaps not even listening; brief dissolves to shots of the lovers together at earlier or later stages of the night punctuate her speech, revealing a wonderfully beautiful rhythm in themselves, but also creating a sense of fragmentation and separateness, a fragile and lovely harmony, never staying constant for long and always on the brink of disruption. The essential isolation of the lovers, the inability of the one truly to reach the other, is ironically counterpointed in the scene of Lena's death at the end of the film, as she slides in a breathtakingly beautiful sweep down a bank of snow and Charlie and Fido stumble towards her body. All Charlie can do on reaching her is to brush the snow and blood from her face; a zoom into her now totally alien and unreachable beauty underlines his loss, yet a dissolve to the face of the new barmaid as he returns to work prepares us for the beginning of a new cycle of hesitation, commitment too late, destruction and loss.

The film is also full of visual devices and jokes, some of them bringing dead metaphors unexpectedly to life: the "two-faced" barman is shown betraying Charlie and Lena in a split-screen shot that catches him in three different postures; one of the gangsters pleads for his mother to drop dead if he is lying and, framed in an antique oval design, an old lady clutches her heart and falls flat on her back, large, clumping boots rising and subsiding as her body hits the floor. The arbitrariness of normal screen conventions and continuity is indicated as Lena holds up a mirror to show Charlie the gangsters following several yards behind them in the street—and their faces loom huge and overwhelming on the screen. Throughout *Tirez sur le Pianiste* Truffaut presents us with a constant tension between spontaneity and stylisation, between what we expect and what we actually see on the screen, and the incongruous rhythms and bizarre juxtapositions force a continual process of readjustment on the viewer as he watches, yet leave him at the end free to make his own application of what he has experienced.

*       *       *

*Charlie meets the new barmaid at the end of the film*

Each of Truffaut's films attempts to solve a different stylistic problem in a different way. The rhythm and movement of the film are shaped by what Truffaut wishes to do with this particular material rather than by the desire to impose a recognisable visual or intellectual pattern on it. There is the sense therefore of a film finding its own way, fulfilling its own needs, triumphantly achieving its own potential. Yet at the same time there is nothing haphazard or totally arbitrary; what Truffaut aims at is neither the disruption of form nor the imposition of his own personal formal structure, but the creation of a new kind of form in which each object (and each person) is free to satisfy the requirements of its own nature. A major

31

method of bringing this about is the undermining of the normal assumptions we make about the way in which actions, objects and responses are connected and inter-related. By upsetting our traditional habits and assumptions he in fact gives us freedom—the freedom to escape from the visual specialisation, the limitation of emotional response to a few habitual, acceptable patterns, which the complexity of our environment constantly forces on us and which most of us unthinkingly accept. In everyday life we tend to see and feel only as much as allows us to find our way without difficulty (and without thinking) through the narrow segment of potential experience we have carved out for ourselves. We thus *recognise* and accept people and things around us rather than *seeing* or investigating them. Truffaut, to put it simply, helps us to become aware of all that we have left out.

Yet Truffaut's films would not make the impression they do if he were not capable of creating, within the new rhythms and new associations which he sets up for us, a formal beauty, a new logic, an inevitability of his own. The success of his films as artistic structures gives us the impetus to attempt to make our own readjustments and the confidence that the attempt is worth making.

In many ways *La Mariée Etait en Noir (The Bride Wore Black)* is the most disconcerting of all Truffaut's films and the one which most critics have been readiest to reject. Yet it is also the most visually beautiful and has a freedom and gracefulness of camera movement surpassed only by *Jules et Jim*. Much of the discontent with the film, in fact, seems to arise from the sustained tension between the cold, self-contained central character, Julie Kohler, and the nature of the intricate, rhythmic dance which the camera performs around her. Except in the scenes with the artist Fergus, where the first hints of self-doubt, of uncertainty about her motives and behaviour come to the surface and are reflected in a more contemplative, immobile camera style, broken into by rhythmically unsettling or shock cuts, the film is one of beautiful grace and fluidity, and the camera seems to flow and glide in patterns of never-ending harmony. This effect is created mainly by tracking shots, but also by a restrained and graceful use of zooms (particularly a subtle combination of pan plus zoom to give an added dimension of movement), together with a perfect blending of the rhythm of camera and background music. The effect is almost literally one of a *dance* in which music and camera combine, the one adapting and suiting itself to the needs of the other. Every major sequence in the film begins with a fluid tracking shot establishing the general locale, then searching out a relevant human figure on which to settle. This recurring movement, with its accompaniment of repeated music motifs, provides a kind of visual punctuation for what is essentially an episodic structure and gives a necessary framework of order and serenity.

The first major episode, in which Bliss is sought out and murdered, opens on a tracking shot of the wall of an apartment building, completely filling the screen and seeming to tower over it at an angle. The camera glides along this, then comes down to isolate and circle round the janitor as he washes the floor of the patio. (This simple-sounding shot has an effect of gracefulness and rhythmic beauty, enhanced by the flow of the music and the serenity of the colour which, quite appropriately, it is impossible to convey in words.) Julie, however, unexpectedly appears from a quite different angle than the movement of the camera would have led us to expect. A very similar effect is obtained in a later episode as the camera follows Cookie and his mother on their way home from school. The child keeps on looking back and the audience assumes that Julie is following them and that the camera is identified with her. The camera continues with them to the driveway of the house, moves forward along the hedge as they vanish from sight, stops, seems to hesitate and move back and forth indecisively, then tracks back to the entrance to the driveway where a ball suddenly rolls towards it along the path; Julie appears and picks up the ball, not from the right of the frame as we would expect, but from the left. It is almost as though the camera were imposing its own order and pattern on the material, and making the audience accomplices in its choice.

There are examples elsewhere in the film of almost abstract rhythmic patterns carried out by the camera: in the first scene in the jail the camera tracks behind the food-cart through the women's corridor; for the first two cells the camera stops and a prisoner moves into frame from within the cell, but at the third cell the camera continues and circles round to the open door to *find* Julie. Exactly the same pattern is created in the men's corridor, where the camera finally circles in to search out Delvaux. The repeated pan plus zoom-out shots of the church spire and down to the wedding group on the steps establish a compulsive visual centre for the film; the harshness and abruptness of the camera movement, together with the blaring incessant music which stops on exactly the same note every time, gives the scene the intensity and crudity of a nightmare from which we, and Julie, are struggling to awake.

One of the most impressive features of the film is the handling of transitions. After Bliss's murder the camera follows Julie's scarf as it floats away over the Mediterranean landscape, seeming to dance to the rhythm of the lute music that accompanies the shot. Movement and sound blend with the exquisite colour and beauty of the scenery to create something close to the purely aesthetic gracefulness of the waltzing spaceships in *2001: A Space Odyssey*. Yet just as in Kubrick's film the aesthetic force comes from the juxtaposition of Nineteenth century music and

Twenty-first century technology, the fusing together of the associations of leisure, idleness and "useless" luxury with those of efficiency, impersonality and dedicated purposefulness, to form a new unity, so in Truffaut's film this scene draws its strength from what follows. The scarf is shown caught on a tree and behind it we see the arc of a jet plane taking off, carrying Julie to her next victim; the camera holds, follows, zooms in on the plane's flight, leaving the scarf behind. The contrast and juxtaposition of free-flowing formal beauty and ruthless single-mindedness epitomises the structure of the film as a whole.

When Julie and Robert Coral, her second victim, leave the concert at which she has arranged to meet him, the camera tracks along the pavement before them as they talk, stops as Julie leaves him, then tracks slowly before Coral as he walks away singing quietly and happily to himself. He then moves towards the camera into blurred close-up and leaves the frame, while in the background the lights go out in the town hall. There is a cut to a flowing zoom in on a row of bottles on a store shelf, as Julie begins her preparations for poisoning him. Another transition, which has been criticised as an example of Truffaut's urge for lyrical effects getting out of hand, likewise gains its full significance from juxtaposition. Cookie's teacher, arrested on suspicion of the murder of his father then released on Julie's intervention, returns to school: there is a medium close-shot of her entering the gate, a partial zoom back to long-shot, then a rapid full zoom to a high-angle crane shot as children pour towards her from all sides of the screen. There is an exhilarating sensation of space, movement, happiness, freedom, which contrasts sharply with a cut to a close-up of Julie in a dark confessional, her face criss-crossed by bars, still bent on imprisoning and enclosing herself in her urge for vengeance, denying herself the freedom she has just awarded another.

Both in details and in the structure of the film as a whole the fluid visual rhythm, the bright, glowing colours, the vivid music provide a vital counterpoint to the static, self-enclosed central figure. The style of the film offers an openness, a responsiveness to the full variety of sensual experience, a graceful harmony—all of which she has chosen to reject. Truffaut puts back into her world, for us to see, all that she has left out of it, and the choice she makes is not so very different in its basic nature from the one all of us make every day in the process of daily living. Only once, and briefly, does Julie join in the dance which is going on around her: as Coral sits and unsuspectingly drinks his poison she dances for him to the music of the mandolin record that she uses to key herself up for each new stage of her revenge. Her partner is the camera, moving with her as she circles the room, and as she becomes more rapt and Coral's mind more hazy, the music begins to change and the screen is filled with superimpositions as the background seems to move in different directions from her and at rhythms of its own, faster or slower than hers. But the visual unity is a forced and transitory one; the dance is soon over and Julie steps out of it back into the world she has chosen to inhabit: Coral, who, like all the other men, had seen in her only what he was prepared and wanting to see (like the others, he focuses his attention primarily on her legs) suffers for his imperceptiveness, and Julie impassively watches him die.

❊    ❊    ❊

In the films dealing with Antoine Doinel, Truffaut's *alter ego*, there is much less virtuosity of style and the camera often seems content to record rather than to create. This is natural enough, given Truffaut's readiness to let each film take on the shape and

pattern best suited to it. *Les 400 Coups (The 400 Blows), Baisers Volés (Stolen Kisses),* and the section of the compilation film *L'Amour à Vingt Ans (Love at 20)* made by Truffaut, which forms a kind of bridge between the two features, are all frankly semi-autobiographical and Antoine Doinel, played by Jean-Pierre Léaud in each case, seems to reflect much of Truffaut's own personality and experience. In each of these films the focus is on fairly ordinary, normal people, on situations, settings and incidents such as everyone has experienced at one time or another. There is not then the kind of barrier presented by the circumstances of the other films: a *ménage à trois* centreing round a woman determined to ignore all conventional moral and social standards; an ex-concert pianist who feels himself responsible for his wife's suicide and determines to cut himself off from all emotional involvement as a result; a woman who sets out ruthlessly and coldly to murder five men. In these films the stylistic disorientation is essential if the audience is to be led to abandon moral and social preconceptions and to understand and sympathise with these people. The freedom we gain from responding to new visual rhythms and associations carries over into our assessment of human behaviour; we are open to a much wider range of experience than before and less inclined to judge on the basis of socially-conditioned reflexes and automatic assumptions. Aesthetic and emotional sensitivity merge with moral and intellectual flexibility.

In *Les 400 Coups* and *Baisers Volés* there is not the same need to bring the viewer into contact with behaviour and feelings which may at first be strange or alien to him. Young love, family quarrels, friendship, injustice, betrayal, happiness, misunderstandings, persecution, loneliness, tenderness—all these

*Previous page: Three faces of Antoine Doinel: Jean-Pierre Léaud as he appears in LES 400 COUPS, L'AMOUR A VINGT ANS, and BAISERS VOLES*

are elements of everyday experience, and instantly recognisable as such. Truffaut does not have to *create* recognition of our affinity with the characters of these films, as he has to with Charlie or Julie Kohler. The focus therefore is on *showing* us the characters, on letting them reveal themselves through their speech, behaviour, gestures, clothes, the settings they live in and move through, the relationships they enter into. Yet this is done with such care, such attention to detail, such respect and love for human beings, that we emerge from the film with much deeper insight and receptivity to the vast potential of human experience. Simply by showing us so much and so fully, Truffaut again takes us away from the narrow track of daily living, shows us how much we leave out, makes us aware of and newly sensitive to the radiant happiness, the inevitable sadness and frustration, the unnecessary misery of the world around us. He increases our capacity for joy, he gives each individual his full worth and value as a human being, and he shows us the cruel and stupid and thoughtless ways in which we destroy both joy and human dignity.

In both films (and in *L'Amour à Vingt Ans*) Truffaut blends comedy and sadness in a way which reflects the unpredictable nature of everyday experience; but the comedy is never cruel and the sadness never sentimental. His comic technique is close to that of Chaplin: the camera tends to observe as people reveal themselves or "perform" before it. Only rarely does the camera "create" the joke, as in *Baisers Volés* where a scene opens with a close-up of the back of Antoine's head as he walks along the street, then pulls back to show him accompanied by a girl a full head-and-a-half taller than he is. Normally Truffaut prefers to set up little scenes such as the gym class on their outing through the streets of Paris in *Les 400 Coups*, the boys gradually drifting away till the master is left with only three to accompany him—the whole scene being observed at a distance by the camera. Or there is the earlier scene in the school room of one of the boys blotting and tearing out page after page of his exercise book until he realises to his horror that he has only two pages left—where the comic effect is obtained through editing, rhythm and timing (the brief shots of the boy being intercut with other activity in the classroom), facial expression and the sheer physical clumsiness with which the child contrives to smear ink over everything in sight. A favourite device used in both films is that of a lingering, expressive fade at the end of a particular "turn," yet this is also rather disconcertingly used to add poignancy to serious, painful scenes.

What is most characteristic, however, is the sense of freedom, vitality and spontaneity that is created, together with the intense involvement with Antoine which Truffaut achieves. This involvement comes less through the normal method of subjective shots—letting us see incidents and people as though through the character's eyes—than through close-ups, which draw us into intimate identification with the figure on the screen. Very few scenes in *Les 400 Coups* are shown through Antoine's eyes; there are some shots from his point of view (mainly upside-down) in the revolving drum in the fairground, and we see the streets of Paris as he does as the police van takes him away to the reformatory, but normally we see Antoine as part of the world around him, and it is the sense of interaction between the boy and his environment that gives the film much of its strength and insight. The close-ups of Antoine's reactions to his experiences, his face by turns puzzled, hurt, joyful, bewildered, shrewd, apprehensive, sly, expectant, bored or desperate help to make us part of him and what he is going through. Several scenes focus almost entirely on his reactions, without sentiment, yet very effectively: his almost expressionless face as he lies in bed watching his mother return late, then hears her quarrel with his father—the very lack of reaction telling us how common this kind of incident is and how he has become outwardly at least inured to it. Or his evident boredom as his mother tries to curry favour with him through irrelevant stories of her childhood. Or, and perhaps most powerfully of all, the long close-ups of his face in the prison van, an almost imperceptible tear finally stealing down his face—a scene handled with impeccable restraint, subtlety and dignity, the very roughness of the technique as the camera lurches awkwardly towards Antoine from a following car adding to its authenticity.

The culmination of this method is the famous scene with the psychiatrist, which focuses entirely on the boy's reactions to his unseen questioner. Antoine's face, the tone of his replies, express almost all we need to know to understand him, yet the quality of the scene would be entirely different without the compulsive movements of his hands smoothing the blotting-paper on the desk before him and the series of unexpected dissolves that seem almost literally to change his personality each time—a process he has had to learn to survive in the world around him.

Involvement through close-up and facial expression relies of course on an essentially static camera, but we also have the typical Truffaut technique of involvement as the camera follows the characters and adjusts to their movements, creating a sense of unpredictability, of a film that reflects the pattern of life and is open-ended. This too can achieve powerful emotional effects, as in the scene where Antoine's lie about his mother's death having kept him away from school catches up with him. The teacher disappears from the class room in response to an unseen summons, the camera tracks in on Antoine's worried face, he is called to the door, the camera tracks in on a close-up of his furious mother (the audience still being prepared to treat the situation as comedy), a close-up of Antoine is followed by the sudden intrusion of his father and a brutal slap that brings the audience up short, the camera follows Antoine back to his desk

*LES 400 COUPS: Antoine sees his father and "dead"
mother at the classroom door . . .*

then tracks in to a close-up of his pained and resentful face,
the image fades. Here the audience's experience and Antoine's
are fully integrated. In the final sequence of the film we accompany Antoine on his run from the reformatory to the sea
in a long tracking shot, we follow him to the beach, the camera
stops as he walks slowly into the water, he turns and walks
back towards the camera, then stands still, and the camera
tracks into the final close-up and freeze-shot that indelibly impress on us our involvement in and responsibility for his fate.

The static camera traps and holds the character at the same
time as it reveals him to us. Escape is associated with movement; Antoine's moments of freedom in the streets of Paris

*. . . and retribution follows. Albert Rémy is the
father, Claire Maurier the mother, and Guy Decomble as the
teacher is between them*

create an impression of vitality and spontaneity, yet the camera
itself moves surprisingly little—as in *Stagecoach* the impression
of movement comes from the activity on the screen and the
sweeping flow of the music. The scenes of most violent camera
movement—those of Antoine stealing then attempting to return
the typewriter—are shot with no musical accompaniment and
have a much greater quality of tension and anticipation than a
conventionally scored piece of mood music could have attained.
In the intermediate scene between these two, as Antoine and
René roam the streets trying to dispose of their embarrassing
acquisition, the camera moves with and follows them to a
certain extent, but the impression of urgency is created again

mainly by the music. We are never distracted by the use of the camera purely for its own sake; Truffaut shows surprising maturity for a first feature in allowing the camera simply to observe so often and for so long, yet his patience enables him to catch completely and movingly a character, a situation and a setting with which we became fully involved.

The whole rhythm of *Les 400 Coups* reflects the patterns, the unpredictability of everyday life, the alternations and overlapping of joy and sadness, pain and hope, boredom and escape that we all undergo but seldom become aware of until we see them revealed for us on the screen. The film seems to fall into a pattern of quickly-edited little cameos, yet this apparently random series of episodes builds up into a cumulative sequence from which there is suddenly no escape (again an aspect of everyday existence which remains hidden from most people who go through it).

Truffaut's episode in *L'Amour à Vingt Ans*, which takes an older Antoine through an abortive and unfulfilled love affair, has the same qualities on a minor scale, the camera catching with painful yet comic accuracy the fumblings of the inexperienced and awkward young man as he tries to cope with his coolly detached girl. Antoine's enthusiastic bunglings win him the amused friendship of the girl's parents but get him nowhere with the girl herself. Again we are given a series of vignettes—Antoine carefully selecting what he thinks is the seat beside the girl at a concert in an attempt to pick her up, then discovering that she is really sitting some rows ahead of him; Antoine clumsily trying to kiss her in a cinema and being expertly repulsed, or moving into an apartment opposite her home and professing great surprise when she and her parents return; or

*Opposite: Antoine (Jean-Pierre Léaud) and Colette (Marie-France Pisier) in* L'AMOUR A VINGT ANS

Antoine finally left to watch television with the parents as the girl goes out for the evening with a new boy friend, the three of them firmly turning their backs on the traitress in a gesture of fine solidarity. The film takes its quality from the accuracy, the tenderness, the sympathy with which the enthusiasms, disappointments and misunderstandings of young love are portrayed and captured; its rhythm reflects perfectly the alternations of progress and setback, false hopes and real achievement, and the final juxtaposition of Antoine's desertion and a series of stills of other, more successful lovers has the typical Truffaut quality of elegiac honesty, of being both an end and a beginning.

In *Baisers Volés* Antoine is older still, but no more self-assured or competent at coping with the problems of everyday living. This film has a quality of radiant happiness that makes it one of the most beautiful accounts of human experience ever placed on the screen, yet it has also compassion, understanding, an undercurrent of sadness, betrayal, loneliness and death which gives it a disturbing and moving complexity. All these elements are fully integrated and their interaction, the way in which they play off against each other throughout, make the film a sudden illumination for the audience, a revelation of the potential of human experience and the unnecessary waste of that potential.

*Baisers Volés* gives an impression of complete yet effortless control on the director's part, the film seeming to find its own way (much of it was improvised with little or no set script) yet moving with inevitability and certainty. This results from a fusion of acting, setting, colour, attention to detail, a flair for comic situations and response, respect for people, and an ability to make the camera do exactly the right thing at the right time for the right purpose. As in *Les 400 Coups* the focus of the film is on people, and they can often best be created by allowing the camera simply to watch and investigate them. So Truffaut is prepared to film two longish conversations, that between the head of the detective agency and the magician's friend and that between the former and M. Tabard, in the conventional but functional manner of alternating close-ups of their faces (and hands) as they speak, letting the characters reveal themselves through facial expression, words, intonation and gestures. Yet the film also has a beautiful rhythm, created by editing and timing rather than by the ceaselessly gliding camera of *Jules et Jim* or *La Mariée Etait en Noir*. The pace is gentle and leisurely, typical camera movements are slow pans and unhurried tracking shots, but cuts are often deliberately abrupt and unconventional (the army officer moving briskly from right to left in one shot, then from left to right in the next), establishing the general chaos of Antoine's existence, yet, as in *La Mariée Etait en Noir*, given an overall sense of continuity through being linked by recurrent musical motifs.

Stylistic coherence is also strengthened by the repetition of certain visual motifs, such as those of hiding and following. Antoine is first glimpsed hidden behind a book in the military prison; as a detective he hides from view behind a newspaper (held upside down, of course), then dodges about behind trees in a vain attempt to keep out of sight; he slinks from doorway to doorway as he follows the magician home from work; and in the scene where the workers in the detective agency try to find out whom Mme. Tabard had been to visit early in the morning, Antoine is blocked from view by his boss's figure until he ruefully emerges to make his confession. In the images of following, the camera joins the characters and interacts with them; the blending of the two types of movement often creates moments of tension and uncertainty that undermine or infiltrate the surface relationships. At certain stages of the film it begins to look as though no one is doing anything except trail someone else around Paris: Antoine is following M. Tabard, Mme. Tabard is following Antoine, a woman detective is following Mme.

Tabard. As far as Antoine is concerned, the whole business is fairly light-hearted, but a note of unease is injected early in the film by the revelation that Christine is continually being trailed by a strange man—first seen conspicuously isolated in the corner of the frame by a masking shot which widens out to take in the object of his pursuit. Later, as Antoine and Christine walk through the park, quarrel, and separate in anger, the camera tracks in front of them as they talk, revealing the stranger as he crosses the frame in the background, unseen by them, and vanishes; Antoine goes off, there is the sound of footsteps, then silence, Christine too moves away and the camera tracks with her; behind her the man enters the frame and the few notes of music constantly associated with him are heard. The sense of unease established by repeated movements of this kind begins to pervade our whole response to the Christine-Antoine relationship. When Christine leaves Antoine's apartment, having failed to get any reply on the morning when Mme. Tabard succeeds in seducing him, the stranger again appears behind her in the street and as he leaves the frame we see the woman detective who has been trailing Mme. Tabard. The effect is simultaneously comic and unsettling. The motives of the stranger's pursuit are finally explained at the end when he approaches Antoine and Christine together, makes a profession of love to her, and says he will continue to love her always, that he knows that one day soon she will turn to him, and that he will wait for her knowing she will not betray him. Antoine and Christine move off, puzzled and slightly angry, yet amused too, happy in the confidence that their own love will endure. They walk away through the tree-lined square, the music on the soundtrack is that of the love-theme, but the last shot of the film injects a sombre note into the lyrical effect by showing the man doggedly following after them. The motifs of hiding, following and pursuing help to give unity and continuity to the

*The fight in the agency office in BAISERS VOLES:*
*Antoine tries to help subdue the conjurer's friend (Simono)*

visual structure, but the associations of suspicion, distrust and
secrecy which they arouse also create considerable ambiguity,
especially around the apparently happy ending.

As in *Les 400 Coups* the few moments of violent activity in
this essentially leisurely film are created through cutting, music
and sound rather than by hectic camerawork. Antoine loses his
first job, as a hotel receptionist, through allowing a private detective and a cuckolded husband into the room occupied by the
unfaithful wife and her lover. The camera follows the two men
into the hotel, pans desperately with the distraught Antoine as
he rushes to find the key and take them upstairs, but once in
the hotel room the effect of movement is created through rapid

cutting, agitated music and the movement of the characters within the frame, with the occasional hurried pan-shot. A similar technique is used in the struggle in the office of the head of the detective agency as the magician's friend refuses to believe in his betrayal. The comic technique is essentially that of the camera watching behaviour and reactions, though some of the best visual jokes are created by the camera—which tracks, for example, along the line of parcels as Tabard goes through the motions of "choosing" an assistant, reveals that Antoine is doing pretty badly, moves up to face level and tracks back again, showing the confidence on the faces of the others and the distress of Antoine, then tracks along again with M. Tabard as he investigates the results and selects the shambles created by Antoine as the most proficient—and the shot freezes on their embarrassed faces. One of the most beautiful shots in the film employs the "searching" motif prevalent in *Jules et Jim* and *La Mariée Etait en Noir* as Antoine, alone in M. Tabard's shoe shop after hours, seems to be drawn by a woman's singing to look for Mme. Tabard, the camera tracking subjectively and falling into an exquisite visual harmony with the rhythm of the music, as he searches, hesitates and at last finds. This element of "finding" is strong in a film which is concerned mainly to reveal rather than to transform, though the qualities of insight, honesty and compassion in it make the world we return to immensely richer and more vibrant.

✿　　✿　　✿

*BAISERS VOLES: Antoine discovers Mme. Tabard (Delphine Seyrig) in the shoe shop late at night*

It is characteristic of most of us that we rarely understand what we think we "know." Familiarity and routine deaden ordinary emotions and experiences to such an extent that most of us rarely feel anything very much in them any longer or have any urge to realise their full potential. It is Truffaut's genius in films like *Les 400 Coups* and *Baisers Volés* to take something like childhood or young love, which we have all gone through and therefore think we "know," and make it live again, or as though for the first time. In films like *La Mariée Etait en Noir* or *Tirez sur le Pianiste,* on the other hand, he takes us into areas of experience that most of us do not know, or prefer not to know, makes these areas available to us, and makes us responsive to them.

*La Peau Douce (Soft Skin)* has elements of both kinds of film in it and therefore poses a different stylistic problem. The situation of Pierre Lachenay is almost pathetically banal: a successful middle-aged, comfortably married, rather complacent literary man falls in love with a glamorous young girl and has a brief and disastrous affair with her. It is a situation most people are familiar with, if not from life at least from literature and television; what Truffaut does with it is, on the one hand to remove the gloss and the dead accretions of *cliché* with which familiarity has surrounded it, and on the other to forestall conventional moral judgements on the characters and their actions by making us share and thus understand their experience. The handling of the film therefore requires both objectivity and subjectivity: the former if we are to see the situation as it really is, not as we have been conditioned through habit to see it, and the latter if we are to be jolted out of stereotyped responses and into a more fully humane viewpoint. All the other films demand some combination of subjective and objective response, but in *La Peau Douce* the balance between them has to be held extremely carefully and by different means.

Editing is more important in this than in any other Truffaut film. The opening scenes consist of a series of very short, quick shots which take Pierre back home, out again, to the airport, to Lisbon, to his hotel, and to the lecture hall. The impression is deliberately fragmentary, with little sense of continuity in place or time; we are continually disoriented by jump cuts and by the restless camera hustling round people and seeming to urge them on whenever the shot is allowed to last more than a few seconds. The effect is rather similar to the opening sequence of *Tirez sur le Pianiste,* with the important difference that the circumstances here are quite clear to us—and the result that the disparity between the ordinariness of the situation and the stridency of the treatment becomes more pointed. These scenes create the basic rhythm of the film and present a world of fairly ordinary concerns, but which is always slightly out of kilter because the characters have no time to pause, to assess their behaviour or to realise the nature and consequences of their actions—the world once more in which we all live and to which we respond in very much the same way, deadening ourselves as far as possible and taking the easiest way out of any emergency, which is simply not to think about it. The sense of fragmentation, of a world that no longer holds together in any meaningful pattern, is heightened by the numerous inserts of hands throughout the film—opening doors, starting cars, changing gears, turning keys, switching lights off and on, picking up suitcases, attaching labels—all suggesting movement, change, disruption, constant activity.

The first shot in the film which is held for any length comes outside the lecture hall in Lisbon as Pierre waits before entering to give his talk, but the disruptive rhythm soon establishes itself again and predominates throughout the first third of the film as Pierre's affair with Nicole, the airline stewardess, gets under way—up to the scene in the service station which takes this element of the style to an extreme in a series of very short shots as Nicole gets out of the car, goes to change her dress, Pierre stands watching the road, the attendant fills the tank (his hands in close-up), and Nicole returns. In the central section of the film, around and just after their visit to Reims, the alternations of tension and momentary reconciliation between the lovers allow for a more objective, detached camera style as we watch the relationship begin to fall apart. This is also paradoxically the most comic section of the film and the emotional tension is counterpointed by some characteristic set-pieces in which we see Pierre struggle to escape from a local bore: trying to see round the other's head and through the window of a café to where the deserted Nicole is being pestered by a man in the lonely street; slipping away from him into the hotel to reassure Nicole that he hasn't forgotten her, then returning to find Clément turning in vague circles looking for him; finally sneaking out of town with Nicole as Clément waits forlornly on the steps of his hotel for the lift to Paris he had been promised. The camera watches these scenes objectively, allowing us to see both the absurdity and the pathos of the situation as Pierre blunders from one mistake to the next yet achieves a few moments of apparent harmony and peace in the midst of the disasters. As usual Truffaut does not allow either us or his characters to fall into any one settled pattern of emotional response for long.

In the last third of the film, however, the editing becomes much more conventionally melodramatic as Truffaut unfortunately makes the mistake of allowing a stereotyped plot structure to take over from the unsettling accuracy and honesty of the rest of the film. As Franca, Pierre's wife, finds out about the affair and begins to make preparations to murder him, Truffaut switches from the creative fragmentation of the first third of the film and the disconcerting conjunctions of the second, to a purely conventional type of "suspense" editing, intercutting Franca's preparations and her journey to the restaurant with Pierre's attempts to 'phone her and his unsuspecting meal. (I almost used the words "Hitchcock editing" here, and of course this kind of cutting is closely associated with the work of Truffaut's acknowledged master, but, in this film at least, Truffaut seems to have learned more constructively from the imposition of a pattern of crisis on mundane people and settings which Hitchcock carries to perfection in a film like *Vertigo*.) Both subject and treatment have the flatness of fulfilled expectations—something one rarely associates with Truffaut.

With the exception of the ending, the editing of *La Peau Douce* helps us to make creative associations between the world of the characters and our own experience and to become sufficiently aware of our affinity with them not to reach for stereotyped moral categories in which to place them. At the same time we are held at a certain distance and encouraged to understand them rather than identify intimately with them. The character on whom we are most likely to pass judgement nevertheless is Pierre, and Truffaut therefore uses the camera in a subtle and rather untypical way to take the audience subjectively into Pierre's experience. He stretches time out or compresses it in the various elevator scenes in the Lisbon hotel in a way that makes us literally *share* Pierre's responses (and so less likely to reflect on the fact that five minutes before, in terms of screen time, he was taking an affectionate farewell of his wife and daughter). The elevator seems to move with painful slowness as Pierre, Nicole and Frank, the airline pilot, go up in it together and Pierre tries to think of some way of opening a relationship with Nicole; it moves much more quickly as it goes down from her floor to his own, the floor numbers now flashing rapidly past; and it proceeds at a "normal" speed as he and Nicole go up together on their return from dinner the next day. When they leave the elevator to go to her room we are again brought into harmony and identification with Pierre through slow-motion shots. When Pierre returns to Paris and is leaving the 'plane and taking what he thinks is a final farewell of Nicole, time is extended in a series of overlapping close-ups (viewing the two of them from different angles and repeating part of their movements each time)—as he would want to extend this moment as far as possible. Later in the hotel in Reims where Pierre is forced to attend an official dinner before his speech, his sense of being trapped is beautifully conveyed in a shot of a line of guests stepping inexorably and apparently endlessly towards him, all looking immensely formidable and aggressive. During the dinner he is told that a young girl is waiting to see him; the news arouses a quite natural curiosity in the guests, who fall silent and look expectantly at him, but Pierre's sense of guilt transforms this into the deathly hush and sharp accusing faces which we see on the screen. And at the end of the film time is stretched out in the moment before his death in the overlapping editing as Franca hurls the incriminating photos on the table before him, conveying both her desire to make him *know* why he has to die and the endless moment of recognition which he experiences. All these succeed in taking us inside Pierre and his reactions by a method unusual for Truffaut, who prefers to create audience involvement through rhythm (as in *Jules et Jim*), close-ups *(Les 400 Coups)*, or detailed interaction between character and environment *(Baisers Volés)*, but which contributes to the authentic and revealing treatment of a hackneyed subject which *La Peau Douce*, despite its ending, becomes.

\* \* \*

It seems strange that Truffaut, whose genius lies in the free, the open and the spontaneous, should be so enthusiastic about and so determined to make a film of Ray Bradbury's *Fahrenheit 451*. Bradbury's novel[15] is intensely moralistic, even self-righteous; whatever sympathies one may have for its plea for the importance of literature and the questioning, individualistic, unconventional habits of mind fostered by it (as opposed to television, which tends to smooth out differences at the same time as it brings men into a closer unity), Bradbury's insistence on presenting his theme as a conflict of black-and-white between cardboard figures who preach interminable sermons at each other completely destroys intellectual validity or tension. Perhaps Truffaut was intrigued at the very incongruity of presenting a defence of literature through the medium which has usurped its central place in contemporary culture, or perhaps his own very deep commitment to literature (evident in all his films and especially *Jules et Jim*) made him disproportionately responsive to the idea of the book and blind to the defects of its treatment. In any case the result is a film that goes wrong in almost every respect and for which Truffaut, who fought for years to make the film and wrote most of the script, must take full responsibility. There is no attempt to change the book in any very radical way for, as in most of his films based on novels (*Jules et Jim, Tirez sur le Pianiste* and *La Mariée Etait en Noir*) he follows the original with a fidelity and a modesty worthy, in this case at least, of a better cause.

*Fahrenheit 451* begins promisingly enough with the credits spoken (no written words appear at all in the film until the legally necessary statement of date and place of filming at the end) over a series of zooms on an endless parade of television aerials, filmed through filtered lenses of different colours. An authentic blend of familiarity and strangeness is created, an atmosphere that Truffaut tried to maintain elsewhere in the film by setting his story of the future (like Godard's *Alphaville*) in a contemporary setting which is only slightly distorted. The opening scenes are handled with crispness and authority: an unknown man receives a 'phone call urging him to flee immediately, a series of jump cuts in on his face establishing a sense of danger and sudden tension; a fast tilt down the exterior of an apartment building catches him as he takes the warning and escapes. A bright red fire-engine is seen leaving a fire-station and racing briskly to the apartments; the firemen enter the man's room and, in a sequence of curtly edited shots, search it, discovering books hidden in various unexpected places. A long-shot shows books being hurled out of a window and falling in graceful slow-motion to the ground. The firemen set up their equipment, don protective suits, and proceed to burn the books. All this is successfully disturbing, not merely through the inherent strangeness of the situation but as a result also of the refusal even to attempt to explain it, the whole episode being treated as something routine and even tedious. Unfortunately, however, Truffaut is not content, as he is in all his other films, to leave to the audience the creative task of adapting themselves to the unfamiliar world presented to them. Like Bradbury he feels the need to take them by the hand: a small boy watches the fire-engine go past and exclaims portentously, "That means there's going to be a fire!" and as the books burn another boy picks one up and looks at it, only to have it seized by his anxious father and thrown on to the pyre—scenes that are both clumsily explanatory and stagily presented, and, in a manner totally alien to Truffaut's normal style, look as though they exist only to make a specific and emphatic point (as indeed they do).

Any forebodings raised by these scenes are quickly reinforced as the film proceeds. Throughout there is a feeling that Truffaut's natural cinematic instincts, his desire for fluidity and spontaneity, are fighting a losing battle against a subject both mechanical and contrived, and though he talks in his *Journal* of the film[5] of his desire not to make it too serious or solemn, he rarely succeeds in achieving this. The film is never allowed to find its own way; the script constantly demands bluntness, explicitness, a preordained pattern that makes little allowance for subtlety or unexpectedness. The insistent moralising constantly runs counter to Truffaut's normal method of allowing implications to emerge naturally from a subject-matter treated with respect for its own sake. Yet one cannot simply ignore the moralising and turn one's attention to other things for without the moral there is nothing left. Apart from fusing two characters in the novel to form the Clarisse of the film, Truffaut respects Bradbury's concept of

*Book-burning in FAHRENHEIT 451*

human beings, again with disastrous results. One of his own greatest strengths is the ability to create people who have vitality, spontaneity, mystery, unexpectedness, yet here he works with crude caricatures, stereotypes without a spark of genuine life in them (and is not helped by the wooden, featureless performances of Oskar Werner and Julie Christie in both her roles). The result is that the bulk of the film is stilted and over-emphatic and elements that one normally thinks of as characteristic of Truffaut are forced to the background, where they become doodles or "touches" rather than integral to the film as a whole (a shot of what appears to be a couple embracing in a garden which turns out to be one man clasping his arms around himself). Elsewhere Truffaut reveals a submerged alienation from the ostensible business of the film by indulging in irrelevant and over-long tributes to Hitchcock, especially in the scene where Montag breaks into the Captain's office and his presence there is intercut with shots of the latter on his way back, creating a totally artificial suspense which dissolves in anti-climax as the Captain enters and shows no surprise whatever at finding Montag there.

The film is not without flashes of visual interest, however. The camera often moves with characteristic grace and fluidity and the repeated shots of people touching themselves and gazing at or kissing their reflections in windows and mirrors convey a vivid sense of sterility and loneliness. The colour is attractive, though used fairly unimaginatively, except for the filtered shots of the credits and the negative colour and insistent repetitions of Montag's dream sequence. Towards the end of the film Montag flees from his pursuers, a tiny figure seen in high-angle long-shot as he dodges through a maze of narrow high-walled streets, and once he reaches safety he watches his own "death" on a television screen, filmed with just the right amount of over-slickness as bullets inexorably find the most visually effective and unlikely targets (such as an isolated street-lamp). But these are outweighed by the sheer clumsiness and heavy-handedness of many key scenes: that in which Clarisse explains to Montag the behaviour of a man leaving information about hidden books outside the fire-station is particularly bad. It is first of all purely obligatory, a laboured preparation for the much shorter scene in which Linda will later leave information to betray her husband; perhaps because of this the actors talk and behave as though they are carrying out an assigned task they want to get over with as quickly as possible, Clarisse's voice droning on tonelessly as the camera focuses desperately on a man behaving with an awkwardness and lack of subtlety that go far beyond the requirements of the script. At times the fault is sheer technical inadequacy: the old lady sitting on top of her pile of books is so obviously *not* burning along with them that the scene, its element of self-conscious declamation already far too strong, becomes absurd; while during Montag's escape from the "flying men," who are supposed to be proceeding under their own power, the ropes attaching them to a helicopter out of camera range are all too visible. The closing scenes with the "book-people" often have dignity and visual beauty, together with some refreshing and long-overdue attempts at light-heartedness, yet they remain on the whole too insistent and didactic, while the final movements at the end of men and women pacing back and forth in front of the camera repeating the works of literature they have now become have an artificiality and contrivance that undercut the ostensible theme of individuality and freedom. Perhaps most symptomatic of what is wrong with this film is the awkwardness of the scene in Clarisse's school where one of her pupils refuses to speak to her: if there is one area in which Truffaut normally never puts a foot wrong, it is the handling of children, yet here the boy behaves with a woodenness, an embarrassment and lack of spontaneity which once again go far beyond what the situation requires. The film is one that rings false in just this way throughout, the work of someone whose gift is for the natural, the spontaneous, the open-ended, not for something contrived and moralistic, directed towards a particular end from its very start and systematically closing off all alternatives along the way.

*Fahrenheit 451* is Truffaut's only attempt to date to make a "closed" film, one that takes us into a alien visual, intellectual or moral world and forces us to accept the conditions of this world for as long as the film may last. The difference between this particular film, however, and any film by Godard, Bresson or Bergman is that in the work of these directors the process is a continually enlightening one; we return from the world of the film to the "real" world to find our concept of the latter modified or even irrevocably altered. A film like *Weekend*, *Mouchette* or *The Silence* changes the world for us, it makes us see and become aware of things we did not know before, whereas *Fahrenheit 451* merely tells us, in a superficially alien setting, things we either know already or do not want to know.

Truffaut's better and more typical films do not so much offer us a different world which then conditions our relationship to the world of ordinary life; rather they make it possible for us to experience *more fully* the world of everyday experience. The style of Bresson or Godard forces us to experience the world as these men see it; they may lay bare relationships and patterns which we were not previously sensitive to, or did not even realise existed, but we are not allowed to *choose* these patterns— they are exposed to us and we can accept them or reject them. Truffaut's style upsets our characteristic patterns of emotional or moral response but, having done so, leaves us with the free-dom and flexibility to select new patterns from the infinite number now opened up to us.

As Truffaut is not concerned to present us with variations or developments of a particular world-view in each successive film, it is possible for each film to take on the visual and rhythmic pattern best suited to it. The sweeping rhythms of *Jules et Jim,* the disconcerting juxtapositions of *Tirez sur le Pianiste* or *La Peau Douce,* the disequilibrium between constant stylistic flow and static character in *La Mariée Etait en Noir* all serve to free us from stereotyped assumptions about the way in which life is or can be experienced; they make us more responsive to all that lies beyond our own range. Visually quieter films like *Les 400 Coups, L'Amour à Vingt Ans* and *Baisers Volés* make us more sensitive to what falls within the range of normal experience; they help to give the ordinary and the familiar the richness which they have lost for most of us. Truffaut has spoken of his conception of the film as a kind of circus[11] and the comparison is an illuminating one: the whole range of human experience from farce and humiliation to high drama and potential tragedy is presented within the space of two hours, in unexpected and sometimes bizarre conjunctions, with a unity and harmony of its own and yet with the unpredictable and unforeseen always lurking in the background ready to destroy the most smoothly polished performance.

Yet the various styles have enough in common to make it impossible to mistake any five minutes from any Truffaut film (except probably *Fahrenheit 451*) for the work of anyone else. He has of course been greatly assisted by working with some of the finest cameramen in the business, such as Raoul Coutard, Henri Decaë and Nicolas Roeg, and especially by Coutard's ability to produce exactly the right kind of visual image for each particular film—rough and grainy for *Tirez sur le Pianiste,* cold and impersonal for *Le Peau Douce,* full of warmth and light and movement for *Jules et Jim,* rich and glowing for *La Mariée Etait en Noir.* All his most characteristic features are present even in his early short *Les Mistons (The Mischief-*

*Makers)*, with its flowing blend of music and visual movement, the camera, as in *Jules et Jim*, sweeping to accompany lovers as they cycle in an intoxicating burst of music and light; its sensitivity to landscape and the relationship of people to place; its mingling of sensuality and a chasteness that respects the privacy and mystery of the deepest emotions; its creation of people who are vital, spontaneous and fully human, and its unsentimental, honest yet tender portrait of childhood; its disconcerting and illuminating juxtapositions (the lovers, embracing each other, watch a praying mantis consume her mate); its love of the cinema and other film-makers (the famous Lumière scene of the gardener and the hose is re-created, the boys watch Rivette and Chabrol's *Coup du Berger* in a cinema, the girl awards her lover *"zéro de conduite"*); above all its freshness, its ability to make us feel that joy and sadness are utterly new experiences, discovered now for the first time.

In a world where adaptability, flexibility, openness and responsiveness to the full potential of actual experience, and the ability to step out of dead and stereotyped patterns of feeling and thinking are essential for survival, Truffaut is one of the most necessary artists we have.

# 2. Hidden Languages

CONTEMPORARY SOCIOLOGISTS AND CRITICS like Roland Barthes[20] and Edward T. Hall[23] have helped to widen the concept of "language" from a purely conscious verbal activity to include all the varieties of non-verbal signals which we are constantly sending out, whether consciously or not, in order to identify and define ourselves and on which we rely more than we perhaps realise to recognise and come to conclusions about other people. Film is particularly well suited to convey and help us to understand these non-verbal languages and Truffaut in particular seems more aware of their existence and importance than almost any other film director. Clothes, furniture, gestures, faces, what we eat and drink, where and how we live are all, in this sense of the word, languages; we are constantly expressing ourselves through them and often find ourselves defined or limited by them. Charlie Koller's piano is the means he chooses to express himself, but it also expresses *him*, defines, controls and constricts him; Julie Kohler's clothes are equally a language, but one she chooses for conscious deception, and her victims die because they cannot read beneath the surface; even the colour patterns of *La Mariée Etait en Noir* form a language and our understanding and appreciation of the film are enhanced if we can read it.

Truffaut's world is one in which places, objects and gestures reveal, and even control, the significance of human behaviour and emotion. In most cases, a perspective within which the viewer is to observe the film is provided by the credit sequence, in which the titles are superimposed on a background of objects central to the action which is to follow. *Les 400 Coups* begins with the camera sweeping through the streets of Paris in a moving car, glimpsing, then seeming to circle round and home in on the familiar outline of the Eiffel Tower. The buildings we see are architecturally undistinguished, but obviously "decent" and respectable; they are photographed so as to cluster together and loom over the screen, but any suggestion of menace is held at bay by the deliberate sweetness and tunefulness of the background music. A cut then takes us into the dirt and squalor of Antoine's school, an atmosphere and setting which the "decent" element of modern society is unwilling to do anything to improve or change. The physical feel and texture of Paris itself become integral to the meaning of the film; without them Antoine's life and story could not be what they are.

The credits of *Tirez sur le Pianiste* are imposed on a shot of the mechanical workings of Charlie's piano, the hammers thudding with mechanical regularity against the strings, creating the slickly banal tune into which Charlie retreats whenever the realities of the world become too much for him. In a very real sense Charlie *is* his piano; he uses it as a means of retreat, escape, defence, oblivion, and the film will show him attempting to escape from what the piano represents for him, and failing. Behind the credits of *La Peau Douce* are hands, caressing, touching, and withdrawing; the film is one in which contact between human beings is limited to surfaces, is never more than, literally, skin-deep. *Fahrenheit 451* begins with repeated zooms on to television aerials, while the normal printed credits are banished. *La Mariée Etait en Noir* shows a printing press turning out hundreds of copies of the portrait of Julie Kohler made by the artist Fergus before his death. The nude picture captures the sensuality and mystery of the woman, while its mass production suggests other elements of her nature, remote and emotionally enclosed, together with her mechanical determination to carry out her chosen task.

The Paris of *Les 400 Coups* is seedy, grubby, even sordid, yet it is filmed with warmth and affection. Antoine's physical environment has helped to shape him, and it imposes limitations on him, yet he has learned to adapt to this with resilience and resourcefulness; given a moderate amount of luck he would have been able at least to survive the consequences of society's neglect and indifference. The film charts, however, the series of misfortunes that combine to push him down a path from which there is no escape, and where even attempts to satisfy society's mysterious requirements ironically recoil upon him. The lighting of the film imposes a pattern of uniform greyness on all the settings, and few alternatives seem to be offered. There is certainly movement and vitality in the restless panning of the camera as it follows Antoine and René in their brief hours of freedom, yet their escape is limited by the physical setting and always ends in the bleakness and cold of early morning or a rainy and windswept afternoon. The streets of Paris seem to lead inexorably back to home, so that it is quite natural for Antoine playing truant from school to encounter his mother and her lover embracing on a busy street corner. There is little sunlight in the film; as the boys race down the steps of Sacré-Coeur the sky is cloudy and the pavement wet with rain; Antoine breaks the early morning ice on a fountain to wash himself in the sludge beneath; and a night spent wandering the streets finds him gulping cold milk in a back alley at dawn, torn posters fluttering on the wall behind him, and finally pushing the empty bottle down a sewer. The bond between emotion or character and setting is perhaps best epitomised at the end of the first day of truancy, when the class sneak emerges from a urinal after spying on them. Despite this, however, the visual setting is rarely depressing; its effect is real and inexorable, but it is at least partially counteracted in the earlier sections by the spontaneity of the camera movements, the actions of the boys themselves, and the gaiety of the music. After Antoine's arrest, the city is seen only by night and through the grille of the police van, and his last glimpse of Paris is of the bars and strip clubs of the Place Pigalle.

A similar atmosphere emerges from the interiors of the film, which convey an almost tactual sense of dirt and confinement. The physical conditions of the school room, dreary and cramped, with desks designed to isolate, restrict and inhibit, and the bleak, inhospitable playground, emphasise not merely the total lack of opportunity or incentive for the pupils, but also the utter hopelessness of the task set before the teachers, who seem to have retired long ago into a mixture of weary cynicism and resentment. Inside the class room Truffaut concentrates on the physical element of torn and blotted exercise books, chalk squeaking on blackboards, walls that stain rather than come clean with washing. Once again the depressing nature of the setting is partially relieved by the humour with which most of the incidents are filmed and by the fact that most of the boys have retained some element of independence and initiative despite their surroundings; but the comedy of the earlier scenes is steadily muted as the film proceeds.

The physical (and, by implication, the social and moral) aspects of the school setting are echoed in the reformatory. In both cases the children are expected to respond obediently to whistles and to form ranks and troop dutifully into the building, where they are herded into constricted spatial patterns. Given a few minutes of freedom, school children and reform school boys break out into the open in the same way, with a burst of shouting and noise, arguing, fighting and playing leapfrog. The parallel is carried further in that the only physical violence offered to Antoine in the course of the film comes in the two slaps he receives—one in the school and one in the reformatory. An impression is powerfully built up, solely through visual means, of school and reformatory being practically identical, with the one merely a preparation for, or extension of, the other.

*The reformatory recalls the patterns of school in LES
400 COUPS. Antoine waits to be marched off with the others*

Antoine's home provides little contrast to either of these two
settings. His relationship with his parents is created as much
in terms of the spatial relationships of kitchen, living-room
and bedroom, as it is through speech or action. Antoine's bed
is set up in the hallway, with the result that his parents find
him a physical obstacle when they want to enter or leave the
house, just as they find him an obstacle or a nuisance simply for
existing. The paper-thin walls allow him to hear every detail
of their quarrels, so that he can never escape sensing the
antagonisms and resentments that control their relationship.
He sleeps in an old sleeping bag, in torn underwear, and is
dressed in the same worn jacket every time we see him. These

*LES 400 COUPS:
Antoine scrapes out
the rubbish before
going to bed*

things change when his mother attempts to bribe him into
keeping silent about her infidelity: he is allowed for one night
to sleep in his parents' bed and his mother for once touches
and caresses him as she washes him and puts him to bed.
(Normally she does not even kiss him goodnight, merely offering him a bored "Bon soir, bon soir.") The scene, with the
naked boy being towelled dry by his mother, is a vivid reminder of Antoine's ambiguous status, not merely within the

family, but also in society as a whole, on some occasions being treated as an adult, on others as a child, with no consistency or rationale behind either attitude and with no indication for him as to which to expect. Normally, however, Antoine is considered as an unpaid servant, expected to set and clear the table, light the stove, and take out the garbage, and Truffaut creates a powerful physical and emotional effect from the tactual unpleasantness of the hot and dirty stove and the oozing rubbish which the boy has to scrape from the bin.

Despite all this, there is a strong sense throughout the film of the potential for a better relationship within the family. This comes out most strongly between Antoine and his father, though it is never put into words (interestingly, when the mother tries to form a verbal relationship with the boy, telling him about her own childhood and her earlier misdeeds, the only response which she, quite properly, receives is one of polite boredom and disbelief). When Antoine starts to write out his punishment on returning from school, then hears someone at the door, he waits to make sure that it is his mother before hiding his books and re-setting the table. Presumably his father, less obsessed with the proprieties and with getting on in the world, would have been less offended at the boy's "disgrace." With the mother out of the way for the evening, the two males can behave in a less restrained way, simply but effectively created through Antoine's solemnly handing his father a seemingly unending stream of eggs to cook, by the father's breaking one of them awkwardly and cursing, and by the boy's laughter. There is not even this small hint of a possibly better emotional relationship with the mother, however. The only way the boy can relate to her is physically, in admiration of her beauty, and we have the short scene of his handling, almost with awe, the mysterious objects—tweezers, pincers, make-up—on her dressing table.

*Antoine investigates his mother's dressing table*

The jail completes the series of interlocking patterns provided by home, school, and reformatory. It is too cramped, dingy, and badly-lit, and the only conditions it can provide for human beings are isolation and confinement. Our emotional response is conditioned by the brusque physical handling that Antoine receives in the police station—there is nothing overtly cruel or sadistic in it, and this makes it all the more appalling. It is shown to be normal that a bewildered and frightened young boy should be arbitrarily pushed and pulled and hauled about, and that no one should think it worthwhile to try to explain things to him or to make them easier for him in any way. The physical unpleasantness is once again summed up in almost tactual manner by the stress on the dirtiness of the fingerprint ink, which Antoine has no way of cleaning off, and his instinctive shrinking from the blinding light of the flashbulb as his photo is taken. And his uncertain status in the adult world is revealed in the way in which he is allowed to remain in the same cell as a hardened male criminal, but removed to a cage of his own the moment three prostitutes are brought to join them.

Other interiors in the film seem to provide possible refuges or escapes, but each in turn fails. The revolving drum at the fairground allows Antoine a brief escape from the physical restrictions of ordinary life (he turns himself sideways and upside down, while the adults remain frozen upright against the wall), but it disorients as much as it exhilarates. René's home has a faintly sinister air around it, created partly by the gloomy, unwieldy furniture, the stuffed horse and the darkness, but also by the quiet, furtive movements of René's mother, the silent remoteness of his father, and the fact that the two clearly arrange to avoid meeting each other as much as possible. The printing shop in which Antoine is supposed to spend a night away from home in safety turns out to be noisy and uncomfortable, and he is in constant danger of discovery. Eventually he is forced to leave and spends the night wandering the streets.

Even nature does not provide the traditional and expected final escape. Certainly Antoine achieves a few moments of freedom and fulfills his dream of reaching the sea, but the countryside he runs through is bleak, muddy, and uninteresting; the sea itself is an estuary rather than the open ocean, and is dull and grey; the sky is overcast, and the tide is out. And yet even this is not depressing; however muted the ending may be, Antoine has not given up, he has not allowed society and its demands to destroy him, and we as audience have shared in his brief escape from spatial restrictions and enclosure into movement and activity. He slows down as he reaches the water's edge, goes in a little, then turns to face the shore, trapped by the camera, his pursuers, and the audience in one of the most moving last shots in all cinema.

✿    ✿    ✿

*Antoine at the end of*
*LES 400 COUPS*

In *Les 400 Coups* the city is ultimately restricting and confining, but it allows for tentative escapes and explorations and for moments of warmth and companionship. The area in which the film is set is full of the externally decrepit yet reassuring and familiar architecture typical of the city as a whole. In *La Peau Douce* the emphasis is placed on white, stark, angular modern buildings such as Orly Airport or the unfinished apartment building where Pierre hopes to set up house with Nicole. There is very little sense of the city as a whole, or even of the overall atmosphere of one particular area. Whereas Antoine's world (apart from the office where his father works, which has to be reached by *métro*) is relatively homogeneous and can easily be covered on foot, a car being used only for special occasions such as a trip to the cinema, the world of Pierre Lachenay is spatially disrupted and fragmented. Almost all travelling is done by car (one of the main themes of the film being the way in which modern transport hinders rather than aids personal communication), and we are deliberately given no sense of the relative positioning of Pierre's apartment, his office, his restaurant, Nicole's apartment, the airport, and so on. The world of the film is almost completely anonymous in terms of space and of architecture: the coldness and impersonality of the environment reflect the emotional coldness of the characters, and the world they live in is one based on transience, on constant movement from one place or activity to another. There is no sense whatever of nature as even a potential refuge; theirs is a totally urban existence, and the nearest the lovers come to an idyllic pastoral setting is a night in a suburban motel.

Above all *La Peau Douce* is a film of surfaces, and the visual, physical surfaces of the objects offer an image of remoteness and sterility which inexorably involves and reflects the characters. The credits show hands briefly touching and caressing;

this image is caught up later in the film as Pierre watches Nicole lying on the motel bed and gently and sadly caresses her sleeping body. The two can meet on a physical, external level, but neither is capable of a deeper involvement. Of the three central figures, only Franca shows a potential for emotional depth and passion, but Pierre constantly throws up barriers to keep her at a distance—when she meets him at the airport on his return from Lisbon, their relationship is imaged by the glass window which separates them and through which they kiss. In other situations Pierre takes care to detach himself physically from Franca as much as possible, yet yields quickly to her touches and embraces.

The characters, however, are deliberately less interesting than the implications which Truffaut draws from their behaviour. The film is a powerful reflection of the emotional coldness and sterility of contemporary life, where feelings become detached and externalised and touch is merely a signal for sexual desire. The feelings of the characters are so deadened that intentions have to be signalled by means of clothing. Franca has to indicate passion to Pierre by wearing the conventionally seductive black underwear; Nicole sets off for the weekend in bohemian jeans and blouse, but her lover's horror forces her to change into a white dress and conform to his desire for clean, respectable adultery. Roles of mistress and wife are thus inverted, the former being associated with chastity and even frigidity and the latter with sexual excitement and challenge. Pierre meets all eventualities—work, guest lectureships, and adultery—safely armoured in his business suit and tie.

Pierre and Nicole are constantly in movement, each hurrying from one appointment to the next, with the result that they never have any time to stop and get to know each other. Nicole's profession—she is an airline stewardess—enables her to reverse the usual male-female roles in their relationship. It is she who is here today and gone tomorrow, and who does not want to make ties or to commit herself, while it is the man who wants marriage and stability. Truffaut also lays great stress on the role of cars as forces that separate human beings while appearing to join them. The constant close-ups of hands changing gear help to create an atmosphere of constant movement, hurry, and fragmentation. But more than this, they build up a sense of routine and habit, of mechanically carrying out a series of gestures, which spills over into the emotional atmosphere of the film. Paradoxically, the affair between Pierre and Nicole becomes tedious routine even before the lovers have come to know each other properly. They go through the motions of a love affair, but each meeting is so brief or unsatisfactory that it leaves nothing to build on for the next meeting. They have no time to settle down, and most of their time together is spent simply trying to find somewhere to be alone. Each meeting is achieved in an atmosphere of impersonality, hurry, anxiety, and sordidness that leaves them ready only to quarrel with each other the moment they are finally left together.

Throughout the film states of mind are reflected in the setting or externalised in movements, gestures, glances, touches, facial expressions, clothes and positioning. In the hotel in Lisbon after he has succeeded in making an appointment with Nicole, Pierre returns to his room, switches on every possible light and throws himself contentedly on the bed. He has reached for the moment a state of tranquillity and harmony, and in reaching it displays physical vitality or enthusiasm for almost the only time in the film. But he will have to turn off the lights to go to sleep, and anticipation will prove to be much more satisfactory than fulfilment. When he returns home after this journey and is surprised by his wife as he tries to 'phone Nicole, he reacts with a mixture of guilt and aggressiveness. As they prepare for bed, they move through the house switching the

*LA PEAU DOUCE: Nicole (Françoise Dorléac) tries to hear Pierre's lecture at Reims*

lights in one room off and those in the next on as they go. The fragmentary pattern of light and dark created on the screen reflects beautifully the tension and imminent disruption of their relationship.

In the three restaurant scenes with Nicole and Pierre the emotional relationship is created by means of the positioning of the two people. In Lisbon, at dawn, we see the two of them alone in the room, very close together, with Nicole leaning admiringly towards Pierre as he talks about his writing. He responds to her hero-worship and he can feel at ease because he has no fear of being recognised. Later, in Paris, when the affair is still relatively fresh, they dine together. Nicole wants to dance, but Pierre doesn't. He persuades her to dance by herself and watches admiringly as she moves smoothly and sensuously among the other dancers. The physical separation, however, reminds us that the two move, almost literally, in different worlds, in terms of age, interests, and pleasures; Pierre now becomes the passive admirer of someone who is essentially impossibly remote from him. This scene comes shortly before the fiasco of the Reims weekend. Later still, as the relationship is beginning to disintegrate, though Pierre is unwilling or unable to see this, they have dinner again. This time they are separated physically by the table between them and Pierre is nervous and uneasy, afraid that they will be overheard or recognised. Nicole too is uneasy, she talks slightly too loudly, Pierre tries to make her keep quiet, and they lapse into sullen hostility.

Pierre throughout is created almost entirely by means of facial expressions, gestures and vocal intonation. In company, dealing with situations or people he is used to—family, friends, audiences—he is self-assured, authoritative, and controlled. Faced with unexpected problems he becomes a mixture of anxiety and smugness, alternating between self-deprecating little smiles, and gestures like the complacent folding together of his hands when he receives the book of matches with Nicole's 'phone number in it. He is at his worst when the self-doubt and the complacency combine, as, on leaving his flat after the false reconciliation with Franca, he responds to her offer of a painting with a shrug of the shoulders, a wave of the hand, and a muttered "Mais non!" She reacts with admirable and characteristic decisiveness by throwing his suitcase through the doorway after him and slamming the door in his face—though this brief moment of humour is typically counteracted by a shot of her leaning back against the door and sobbing.

Truffaut's concern for detail, however, backfires to some extent at the end of the film. Franca's shooting of her husband in a crowded restaurant at lunchtime is based on an actual newspaper report and is not in itself improbable. Truffaut also attempted to prepare the audience for this *dénouement* by a short scene showing Pierre and Franca out shooting together, but this was omitted in the final cut of the film. Psychologically the ending is justified and has been carefully anticipated and prepared for. What goes wrong really is that Truffaut refuses to cheat. Cinematic convention allows a jealous wife to eliminate her husband by having a revolver handily lying around the house and letting it come to hand at the right moment. Audiences would probably accept an incident of this kind without question; what disturbs them is the sheer bulk of the weapon Franca chooses and the improbability of her carrying it through town and into a restaurant unnoticed. Paradoxically, however, the latter situation is in fact more likely in relation to real life, while the former convinces only because it is a well-established convention (people like Pierre and Franca would be far more likely to have a shotgun in the house than a pistol). Truffaut chooses "real" probability over "cinematic" probability here, just as in the film as a whole he stresses the elements of an adulterous love affair (where and how to meet) which the film conventionally ignores. He plays fair too by showing us a full-length shot of Franca with the gun under her coat and the tip just protruding at the bottom; he shows her getting out of her car and having to rearrange the weapon in doing so. All this should convince, and yet, somehow, it doesn't. Sometimes illusion succeeds better on the screen than truth, as Godard brilliantly demonstrates in the various "killings" of *Bande à Part*. Truffaut's very honesty lets him down here, combined with an extraordinarily inept piece of cutting which shows the diners in the restaurant rising to their feet in unison a second after the shot is fired. This last element strangely parallels the only other piece of unconvincing detail in the whole film, where the passengers wait for the 'plane to come to stop on landing in Lisbon before rising in a body to leave.

\* \* \*

*Tirez sur le Pianiste* shares with *Les 400 Coups* an almost entirely Parisian setting, with a move into the countryside for the ending. But the Paris of the film, like that of *La Peau Douce*, is very nearly anonymous. There is plenty of travel and movement, but through streets which have little character of their own and where the interrelationships of the bar, Charlie's room, Lena's flat, the younger brother's school, and so on, are not clearly defined. The anonymity, however, is that of dark, almost sordid back streets rather than the harshness and barrenness of functional contemporary architecture. The specific settings are rarely *placed,* in the sense of being related to the environment around them. Characters are followed or pursued through streets which have no beginning or end and seem to be cut arbitrarily out of the total setting. At best we see one or two houses to either side of an entrance, or we follow the characters up a stairway and see doors to either side; otherwise the rooms in which the characters live and work seem to exist in a vacuum. This is of course the ideal setting for Charlie, with his desire to retreat into a shell where no one will recognise him and he will need to make no commitment to anybody—once again environment both expresses and shapes the interior movement of the characters. It is not until well into the second half of the film, after Charlie's earlier history has been related in flashback, that the bar is clearly and specifically placed in relationship to the area around it: after a shot of a junkyard full of wrecked cars the camera pans to take in the bar Charlie works in, linking the two visually and emotionally.

The world of the "present tense" of the film creates a closed environment from which Charlie has to escape physically if he is to redeem himself. At first sight the world created in the flashback seems to offer a deliberate contrast in sophistication and glamour, yet visually the two settings have a great deal in common. Charlie's world of fame and fortune is constricting and enclosed; it has an almost unreal quality about it, created largely through the lighting. Almost all the scenes in this section of the film are interiors—café, hotel room, audition, concert hall, press conference, the office where Lars Schmeel the impresario talks to Charlie/Edouard about his future (the lighting in this scene making the city seen through the office window look totally unreal). The implication rises inevitably from this that even in his "good" times Charlie moves in a world of his own and never really relates to other people. Even as a successful pianist he uses the piano as a barrier behind which he shelters or hides—an idea vividly conveyed in a shot which has the piano cover two-thirds of the screen with Charlie's expressionless face squeezed into the triangle left in the top right-hand corner.

The use of corridors in the flashback sequence increases the sense of unease that the other elements of this part of the film convey, and intensifies the feeling of a closed environment with no discernible exit for the characters. The most effective scene in this respect shows Charlie on his way to his audition, moving uneasily along a seemingly endless corridor. He walks in a jerky, hunched-up, almost unco-ordinated way, wearing a coat much too large for him into which we feel he will vanish the moment things begin to get difficult and he needs to escape. He looks pathetic, comic and vulnerable, all at once, and the hand-held camera that tracks back in front of him, tilting and rocking the frame slightly as it moves, crystallises these essential elements in him. When he at last summons up enough courage to ring the bell and enters the room he is replaced by a girl carrying a violin who begins to walk away from the door down the corridor. The camera unexpectedly chooses to follow her rather than Charlie; it tracks smoothly away in front of her and we hear Charlie strike the first few confident notes on the piano. Still we accompany the girl, however; her face is tense and strained, she clutches her violin tightly and awkwardly, and a sense of unease and puzzlement is created at the time we should be sharing Charlie's apparent triumph. There is a cut; we expect at last to join Charlie, but instead we see the girl again, crossing a courtyard with buildings surrounding her on all sides. She stops and looks upwards as, totally unnaturalistically, the sound of Charlie's playing swells louder around her. By filming the turning-point of Charlie's career in this way, Truffaut creates a vivid sense of how fragile and temporary the *façade* which he is creating will turn out to be.

Corridors are used very effectively in most of the other films—in *Les 400 Coups,* where the full significance of Antoine's arrest is brought home by the shot which suddenly silhouettes the bulk of a policeman at the end of a corridor standing behind a barred gate, and in *La Peau Douce,* when Pierre wanders sadly down the hotel corridor after leaving the elevator and missing the chance to ask Nicole out. Again the camera tracks back before him, and the focal length and the lighting create a subtle spatial distortion which reflects mood and state of mind, emphasised by the accompanying shots of shoes, usually in pairs, arranged neatly outside the doors. The scene is paralleled shortly afterwards as Nicole and Pierre return after their evening out and walk slowly back towards her room. In *La Mariée Etait en Noir* the corridors of the jail in the final scene are used to create, not so much mystery and suspense, as a feeling the inevitable accomplishment, as the food-cart jolts down them, doors open, and people appear and disappear, till finally

the camera is left looking stolidly down the empty passage-
way as the climactic murder is accomplished off-scene.

The city in *Tirez sur le Pianiste* is balanced by nature to
some extent at the end, but here too Truffaut refuses to ro-
manticise the countryside. Nature is cold and neutral, the cot-
tage the Saroyans are hiding in is squatly and almost absurdly
isolated. The approach to the hide-out is shot so that the
countryside itself is rarely seen: with the two gangsters focus
is placed almost entirely on the interior of the car and their
conversation with Fido; with Charlie and Lena, Truffaut and
Raoul Coutard create an almost abstract pattern of streetlights
and then falling snow on the smeared windshield. Nature of

*Truffaut (at left) sets up the snow scene near the end of TIREZ*
*SUR LE PIANISTE, with Marie Dubois and Charles Aznavour*

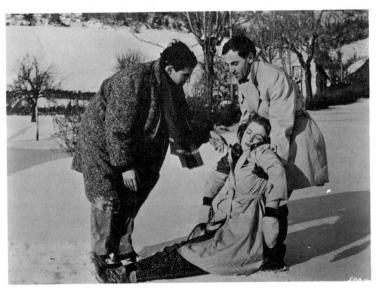

course provides no escape: Lena is shot and left to die in the snow; Charlie reaches her too late and can do nothing except brush blood and clinging snow from her face. The two sets of crooks exit in a farcical chase to continue their meaningless and absurd hostility, and Charlie is left back almost exactly where he started.

Nature provides a more positive alternative in *Jules et Jim*, but here too it fails ultimately because it is treated simply as an escape. Jules and Catherine try to cut themselves off from the world after the War; they isolate themselves physically in their chalet, but they are still near enough to village and railway station that the outside world can and will find them. This is only the most extreme, however, of a series of attempted escapes to the countryside which the characters carry out throughout the film—to the seaside, to the forests and lakes of Germany, and to the river and converted mill of the French provinces. But each time they fail to achieve the serenity, solitude, or harmony they are seeking. In the scenes at the seaside they seek happiness in physical movement—cycling, running and swimming. The movement of the characters is complemented by the movement of the camera, creating a sense of restless, almost nervous exuberance, and leading finally to physical and emotional exhaustion. In Germany the camera does most of the active movement, circling and swooping round the house and its inhabitants, reflecting perhaps the disparity between the happiness assumed by the characters and the emotional tensions beneath the surface—from which they escape once more into bursts of physical activity. The sense of the real change taking place beneath the rather frenzied surface is best conveyed in the quiet restraint of the long scene in which Jim follows Catherine out into the night and they walk and talk together in the darkness, or in the walk that the group take together to the lake in the mist, the mood being created

by the music, the heavy, louring atmosphere, the slow movement of the characters, and the fact that they are filmed in
extreme long-shot. In the scenes at the mill and the riverside
towards the end of the film the action becomes much more
static and a sense of tension and anticipation hangs over everything which is said or done, reflecting the move in the rhythm
of the film as a whole from the creation of meaning through
physical exuberance to the attempt to probe the emotional and
social consequences of the characters' actions.

Paris once again provides the urban setting for the film and
a sense of the pre- and immediate post-War period is vividly
created, yet this is achieved through an extremely selective and
limited use of locales: cafés, rooms, a theatre, a bridge, a few
streets, a riverbank, and some exteriors of houses (especially
one with a distinctive double stairway leading up to it). A
sense of the city as a whole is created through the use of short
newsreel clips that don't so much blend with the rest of the
film as modestly make us aware of how authentic the re-created
scenes look. Newsreels are effectively used elsewhere for other
purposes; in the War scenes, the stretching out of a standard-
ratio piece of film to fit the Franscope frame creates an unsettling effect of distortion and unreality, while shots of Hitler's
burning of the books help to keep us aware of the rapid passing of time in the last third of the film (from 1918 to the mid-
Thirties) and contribute to the history of film styles and techniques which Truffaut maintains as an undercurrent throughout.
The sense of period is strengthened by the deliberately grainy
texture of the film in the earlier sections and by careful attention to every detail of clothing, furnishings, ornaments, and
background material such as posters, crockery and transport.
Catherine keeps her old love letters in a decorated chamberpot
and tips them on to the floor in order to burn them; the fire
spreads to her long nightgown and is extinguished by Jim in

*JULES ET JIM: Jim waits in a café for Catherine.*
*Jean-Louis Richard, who worked on the script of this*
*and other Truffaut films, sits at the far right*

a scene where fear and anxiety are vividly conveyed through
the physical quality of sound and movement—Catherine's gasps
and muted whispers, the crackling of the flames, the scuffling
of the burning paper as Jim tries to beat it out. Just before
this Catherine has produced a bottle of vitriol destined "for
lying eyes"; Jim persuades her to get rid of it, telling her that
it might break in her case and ruin her clothes, and anyway
she can buy vitriol anywhere ("Really?" asks Catherine, genuinely surprised). She pours the vitriol down the sink and again
sound and movement convey a powerful emotional effect as the
liquid hisses and sends up clouds of steam and Catherine turns
her head away to shield her eyes. The physical texture of sound
and image combine to provide a frightening insight into the

ruthlessness of which Catherine has suddenly shown herself capable.

Catherine is intimately associated with the elements of fire and water throughout the film, the two combining at the end in her death by drowning and burial by cremation. Her body and Jim's are placed in large wooden coffins; these are then conveyed into the flames; we see the bones and ashes emerge; the bones are pounded and placed in urns, which in turn are put inside two ludicrously small coffins; finally two attendants solemnly bear the coffins away and Jules walks sadly and yet somehow jauntily behind them. Truffaut's concentration on the physical element of ashes and bones, and the size and shape of the coffins, creates an impression of the ultimate fragility and vulnerability of human experience; there is a sense of waste and futility, but also release as Jules walks off, alone, but also free for the first time in the film. The soundtrack also expresses a similar mingling of sadness and exhilaration: the narrator tells us how Catherine's final attempt to break the rules was frustrated (she wanted to have her ashes scattered to the winds, but this was not allowed), yet the music is that of Catherine's song and tells us that ultimately, despite all else, the triumph and victory are hers.

❊   ❊   ❊

*La Mariée Etait en Noir* and *Fahrenheit 451* are of all Truffaut's films to date the ones least firmly rooted in a particular place or area. The former, however, is given a focal point in time and space by the constant returns to the shooting on the steps of the church, and this in turn is linked to the childhood memory of Julie and David growing up together in sight of a village church and obviously destined for marriage (this is the only attempt made in the film to give any kind of background

88

or explanation for the central figure; otherwise Julie Kohler appears and acts as enigmatically for us as she does for any of her victims). The film takes us to the Riviera, to Switzerland, and to the French provinces; the settings of the first two murders are filmed deliberately as picture postcards (the Mediterranean coast and an archetypal Swiss small town) and the homes of the victims are placed in a larger spatial context, but with the others Truffaut creates only the immediate environment and it is very difficult to tell just where Morane, Delvaux and Fergus (victims three, four, and five, though Delvaux is in fact the last to die) actually live. This steady closing-in of place and the focusing on the immediate setting in which the

*LA MARIEE ETAIT EN NOIR: Bliss (Claude Rich, at right) with his friend Corey (Jean-Claude Brialy)*

*LA MARIEE ETAIT EN NOIR: the arrest of Delvaux (Daniel Boulanger, at right)*

murder is to be committed seem to reflect the growing obsession of Julie to complete her task no matter what difficulties may be created by others or by herself.

In each case the setting interacts with and reflects the nature of the victim. Bliss, the man-about-town who has decided to settle down at last, lives in a vast block of luxury apartments on the Riviera; Julie can trap him to his death by appealing to his willingness to accept the possibility of an intrigue even on the verge of his marriage. Robert Coral lives in a meagre rented room in a small Swiss town. He hides a bottle of gin in his cupboard, taking care to mark the level of what remains in a futile gesture of defence against the depredations of his landlady. The walls of his room are covered with not very daring pin-ups which have been up so long that they leave marks behind when he pulls them down to replace them by a more chaste but equally ghastly travel poster. He cooks and eats in a tiny curtained-off kitchen and has difficulty keeping the curtains together as he tries to obscure it from the eyes of his expected visitor. Wallpaper and carpet are faded and dingy, and bedspread, curtains and chair-cover are all made out of the same material. Each little detail is noted unobtrusively and swiftly, but they all combine with Michel Bouquet's remarkable vignette as Coral to chart tellingly the pathetic minutiae of this man's uneventful life. Julie can destroy him by appealing to his submerged romanticism, his touching eagerness to make up at last for the waste and futility of his existence. Clément Morane, the successful business man and aspiring politician, leads an existence in which status and obtrusive display are all-important; he has a fashionable house, a staircase with expensive wood-panelling, finely-cut glassware, and unusual table-linen. He judges purely by externals and can be easily tricked into the simple trap in which he dies. Delvaux is seen in a setting only of junkyard and jail; from cunning, stupid, and brutal. He is the one who actually does what little we see of him he shows himself to be appropriately the shooting, his face lighting up in mindless pleasure as he first sets eyes on the rifle. Fergus moves in a world of cultivated bohemianism; his clothes, friends, studio and paintings are all those of a man who has gauged exactly the point to which unconventionality can go and still bring in fame and fortune, and who is shrewd enough not to go (and not to want to go) beyond this. He can respond readily therefore to someone who puts on a *façade* as calculated as his own; what gives the relationship its peculiar interest, however, is the way in which neither can keep up the *façade* completely in the presence of the other, and each begins to discover unexpected

*LA MARIEE ETAIT EN NOIR: Julie (Jeanne Moreau) and Fergus (Charles Denner)*

and disturbing depths in his own personality.

The film could easily have become purely episodic, with only the presence of Jeanne Moreau as Julie to provide continuity. The various flashbacks to the scene on the church steps form one kind of linking motif; another, more purely visual one comes from the use of colour throughout the film, especially red and blue. The blue and white patterned wallpaper in Julie's room in the first scene is repeated in one form or another in almost every episode: the curtains in Bliss's apartment and in Coral's room employ a similar motif, as do Cookie's pyjamas, and blue and white appear again in the kitchen tiles in Fergus's apartment, in his tea cups, and in the apron worn by a woman in the prison kitchen. Like the film as a whole, this pattern has its focal point in the church spire, whose clock face has a design of white figures on a light-blue background, and the result is subtly to reinforce the sense of Julie being unable to escape the memory of the murder and re-living it every moment of her life. Every episode contains, and usually begins with, a prominent splash of bright blue or bright red or both somewhere on the screen: the janitor outside Bliss's apartment building is using a red pail and Bliss has a red face-cloth and a blue towel draped round his bath; Coral's landlady shakes a bright red duster out of a window framed by blue and white shutters; Cookie wears a red sweater and plays with a blue ball, he sleeps in an all-blue bedroom and downstairs in the house are a strange luminous red alcove near the front door and red tablecloth and napkins; the cars in Delvaux's junkyard are either blue, white or red, and he is wearing a blue suit; Julie travels to Fergus's studio in a red taxi and looks at a collection of his paintings, all of them predominantly blue and white with the subjects wearing red dresses; he is wearing a blue sweater on her first visit, on her second a red sweater is lying on the sofa and he has this on when she kills him. All of these help to give a pattern of visual unity to the film, and Truffaut's sensitivity to colour as a vital element in visual harmony and continuity is shown also in such minor details as the use of white and pink in Bliss's party: his *fiancée* Gilberte wears a pink dress, she moves away and Bliss goes to talk to Julie, dressed entirely in white, while we are given a glimpse of pink and white flowers in the background; a woman wearing a pink and white dress then appears, and when Bliss and Julie move out on the balcony her white dress is juxtaposed against more pink flowers.

Jeanne Moreau's clothes throughout the film use no colours other than black or white and are carefully chosen to suit and

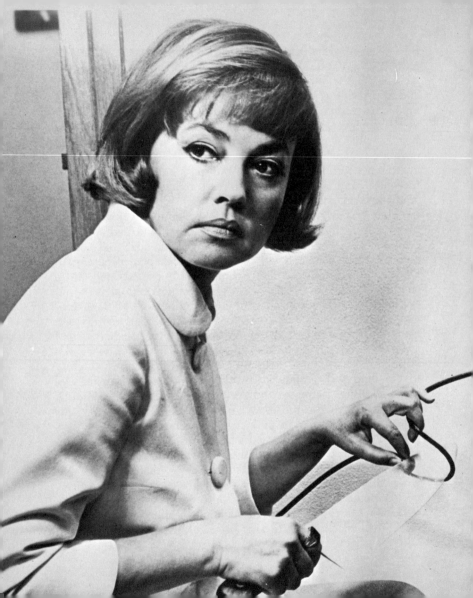

to attract the personality of each victim. For Bliss she wears a white evening gown, creating an impression of remoteness, mystery and glamour which he is particularly ready to respond to as he feels the bonds of matrimony closing round him. When she meets Coral at the concert in the town hall she wears a romantic white cape with a black ribbon and a long sleeveless black dress; in his room she wears a provocative and enticing short black dress. Each appeals to one facet of his personality— the romantic, and the desire to redeem years of loneliness and frustration. For Morane she dresses in a neat white suit to live up to her schoolmistress pretence, but this helps her convey the efficient, businesslike attitude to life and sex that attracts him to her. She also manages to find a black-and-white striped apron in the kitchen! For Delvaux she has a short dress of black leather, a black sweater and black stockings; he is sufficiently interested to give up counting his money only when he hears that someone "who looks like a tart" is waiting to see him. On the first visit to Fergus she wears a white dress, conspicuously without *brassière,* and black gloves; having gained his interest, she switches to a combined black-and-white zigzag motif for her other sittings. As his model, of course, she dresses in white as Diana, goddess of hunting and chastity. Behind all this are the various thematic associations of black-and-white throughout the film: Julie is both a widow and a bride, and we see her dressed properly for each role—in mourning at Fergus's funeral and in white for her own wedding. She is also in her own twisted way a nun with a religious mission to carry out, and we see her dressed in black at the confessional. The various elements of chastity and murder, mourning and religious devotion, death and purity (she is dressed in white as a child in the flashback)

*Opposite: LA MARIEE ETAIT EN NOIR. Julie in her school-mistress disguise cuts Morane's telephone line*

are intertwined throughout the film and Truffaut has probably never used clothes more intelligently or sensitively to create theme and state of mind. What is particularly original is the use of Julie's clothes to reflect, not *her* personality, but that of each of the men. If they had enough self-knowledge to understand what she is telling them about themselves, they would not be tricked by her. This use of clothes to reflect personality, however, raises some interesting problems, for how does Julie *know* in advance exactly what combination of clothes is going to appeal to men whom she has never met before? (It is made clear in the first episode that she does not know what Bliss looks like, and this seems to apply to all the others.)

There are other equally "fortuitous" elements in the film: Fergus has never seen Julie before, yet his gallery and studio are already full of "imaginary" portraits of her. On her visit to Morane, Julie appears at first to have failed to set up a suitable situation for murder (or perhaps her affection for Cookie has brought about second thoughts). She seems to be genuinely on the point of leaving and rejects a perfectly valid opportunity to stay on Morane's invitation, but just as she is about to go out of the door, a totally unexpected (and stagey) thunderstorm starts up and seems to remind her of her "duty"; she comes back in, claiming that she has lost her ring. And at the end of the film she finds herself, quite by chance, housed in the same cell-block as Delvaux and even put on his food detail. The constricted, non-human aura around Julie is increased by the fact that she only once joins in ordinary human activities like eating, drinking and smoking (she has a sip of champagne with Fergus, the only one of her victims she is ever in danger of weakening towards). She doesn't drink the water she asks Corey to bring her at Bliss's reception, nor of course does she share Coral's poisoned bottle (in both cases emptying her drink into a vase of flowers), and though she presumably eats the

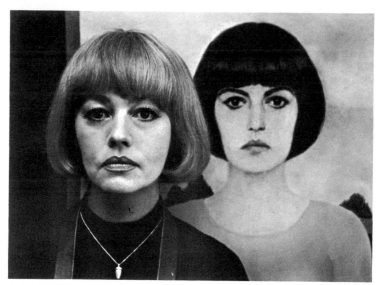

*LA MARIEE ETAIT EN NOIR: Julie and one of Fergus's
"imaginary" portraits of her*

dinner she cooks at Morane's, all we actually *see* is her feeding
the boy at the end of it. All these elements seem intended to
undermine the normal sense of "reality" in the film, and to
give an impression of Julie as being controlled and aided (or
destroyed) by forces beyond human control, but it is an impression very subtly conveyed solely through the visual style.

In *Fahrenheit 451* Truffaut works on a more obvious level of
combining the expected and the unsettling, the strange and the
familiar, presenting us with a world which in appearance is contemporary with our own, yet different enough to remind us
that what we are seeing is a projection of tendencies in today's
world rather than a reproduction of it. He builds his world of
the future out of settings which already exist in the English

*FAHRENHEIT 451:*
*Linda (Julie Christie)*
*discovers Montag's*
*(Oskar Werner's)*
*cache of books*

suburbs and uses the one really unusual feature, the monorail (to be found near Orléans in France), as simply a commuters' tool, part of the daily routine of travelling to work and back. The only explicitly futuristic device is that of the police with their individual flying machines who pursue Montag—one of the few deviations from the book and one where Bradbury's original concept of having Montag flee across an immensely wide highway while a group of sadistic teenagers try to run him down would have suited better Truffaut's blend of the alien and the ordinary. Into this generally familiar world he infuses reminders of the past and anticipations of what to us is still the future: the past in such objects as an antique telephone and a cut-throat razor (reminding us that man can never close himself off completely from his past and that if he refuses to use it fruitfully he will only debase it), the future in clothes, furniture, the huge television screen on Montag's wall. What comes out best from all this is a sense of uniformity, of lack of individuality in both people and places. Private life takes place in a perpetual suburb where the houses all look much the same—this is best caught in the shot which has a row of people stepping almost simultaneously out of a series of identical houses in response to the police demand that they come to their doors to look for Montag. We are never shown the fire-station itself in any clear relation to its environment but what little we see of the city gives an impression of featureless identical streets, walls and houses with flat, regular, monotonous surfaces. All the clothes have the look of uniforms, even in moments of leisure and privacy.

None of this is very original, however; it has been the stock-in-trade of the liberal-humanist critique of the technological, television-ridden world for quite some time now, and Truffaut tends to draw on preconceptions and prejudices here in a way he never does elsewhere, rather than attempting to unsettle or change them. The major situation of the film is therefore presented to us in simple black-and-white terms and elements of visual and intellectual distinction have to be sought for in such background details as a little girl in a park combing her hair with a comb almost as big as she is, or the paraphernalia of the Captain's office, which includes a large bust of himself (he has several others to give as rewards to deserving underlings), a model fire-engine, and a painting of another engine drawn by a horse and cart. Montag and the other firemen wear something reminiscent of priests' robes for burning books, and when Montag gets up to read in secret one night he puts on what looks like a monk's robe (here Truffaut probably achieves best the combination of serious comment and tongue-in-cheek deflation of over-solemnity which he says he sought for). Montag reads by the light of the television set, its programmes closed down for the night; though this is a nice touch, it sparks off some of the embarrassing questions which neither Bradbury nor Truffaut attempt to answer: if Montag has to have the whole concept

*FAHRENHEIT 451: the Captain (Cyril Cusack) explains the evils of reading to Montag after a particularly successful search*

of books laboriously explained to him by the Captain, how does he know how to read? In the same vein, surely a society so dedicated to television at the cost of every other form of entertainment would at the very least have programmes going all round the clock? Moving back to elements which don't pose this kind of problem, there is Linda nervously putting on dark glasses after informing on Montag, and, discovering a hidden book as she is cleaning a shelf, knocking it off with a spasmodic gesture of horror and fear as though it were some repulsive insect. And Montag, ordered by the Captain to burn his own collection of books, turns the flame-thrower first on the beds and then on the bedside television (with its photo of Linda on top of it) in a gesture that explains more than all the dialogue of the rest of the film. But all these tend to be merely compensations for the kind of visual excitement and sensitivity to detail lacking in the rest of the film.

As in *La Mariée Etait en Noir* red and blue dominate the colour scheme, but without the imagination of the later film and with generally a purely functional purpose—the fire-engine is of course red (why not yellow?—that would have been more like Truffaut!) as is almost every detail of the fire-station, while blue is used for the firemen's shirts and for the kerosene in which they soak the doomed books. The vividness of the green countryside through which the fire-engine passes contrasts effectively with the drab surroundings of the book-people, suggesting the difficulties with which they have to contend, and the brightness of the natural colours contrasts with the deliberate flatness of those of the comic books and the television. But these again are ideas which make few demands on either director or audience, and the film as a whole is one that prompts a muttered "of course" and a wise nodding of the head rather than challenging or stimulating us to new patterns of thought and emotion.

*Baisers Volés*, besides taking up the story of Antoine Doinel from *Les 400 Coups* and *L'Amour à Vingt Ans*, also introduces places, objects and even gestures from some of the earlier films. Antoine's room has a view straight on to Sacré-Coeur and in the lobby of the hotel where he briefly works is the travel poster Robert Coral had in his bedroom in *La Mariée Etait en Noir*. One of the hotel rooms has the characteristic blue and white wallpaper of the previous film. At one stage Antoine sits down to write a letter and, exactly as his younger self does in *Les 400 Coups*, he writes a couple of lines speaking the words out to himself, decides he has made a mistake, crumples the page up and begins again. Like *Les 400 Coups* the film begins (except for a credit sequence showing the closed doors of the Cinémathèque Française—the film being made during Henri Langlois's troubles in 1968 and dedicated to him) with a view of Paris prominently displaying the Eiffel Tower, though the picture of Paris presented in *Baisers Volés* is a rather different one.

Antoine's world is now an uneasy combination of the conventional tourist's Paris of sunshine, colour and parks, the seedy hotels and rented rooms where he lives and finds brief sexual satisfaction, the bright plastic world of modern office life, and the comfortable middle-class home of Christine's parents. He moves restlessly between these in the course of the film, never able to settle down in any one of them for long, and constantly running away from what Christine and her family represent for him. The sense of transience is very strong as Antoine moves through a continual succession of army barracks, hotels, cafés, night clubs, offices, shops and other people's homes, unable to establish himself permanently in a setting which is in any case hostile to any attempt at stability. Only Christine's home seems to offer genuine comfort and happiness (as in *L'Amour à Vingt Ans*, Antoine is more at ease and gets on better with the parents than with the girl herself), though the detective agency makes a typically modern attempt at homeliness with a central office full of vaguely Victorian furnishings—faded wallpaper, a huge metal-plated stove, doors with leather padding, heavy gilt-framed pictures and a menacing potted plant. Antoine fears the stability, the inevitable narrowing-down, the routine of what Christine and her family, however attractively, offer him, and the cheap and impersonal brightness of the office where Christine's father works provides a counterbalance to the informality and casualness of their home. The two extremes between which he is caught are vividly and unsettlingly brought home in his accidental meetings with friends he has not seen for years. One, a girl, introduces him to her husband and shows him her baby, and in the group we see Antoine and Christine as they could be, for good or ill, within just a year or two. As well as catching beautifully the awkwardness and slight embarrassment of a meeting of this kind, where the two people no longer really have anything to say to each other, the scene also hints at the hollowness of social forms and the transience of personal relationships as the girl urges him to come to dinner soon without giving him either her married name or her new address. Even more sad and disturbing is the meeting with a young man searching through litter-bins in the street, whether for food or something he can sell, we are not told. Antoine does not question him or stop to talk with him long, perhaps too conscious of how close he himself is to slipping into the same pattern of forlorn rootlessness. He opts for Christine and happiness at the end of course, but the "of course" has much more ambiguity and uncertainty around it than it seems to on the surface.

The feeling of unease is intensified by the context of suspicion and distrust in which Antoine carries out his daily work. For most of the film he is a completely incompetent private detective who cannot even follow a suspect without making himself so blatantly obvious that she reports him to the nearest policeman for annoying her. Truffaut makes much of the way in which Antoine's physical clumsiness throughout the film reflects his emotional inexperience and immaturity. In the fight between the head of the detective agency and the friend of the magician, Antoine's contribution is to fall over his own feet and land sprawling on the floor. In his job as a television repairman he manages to crash his van into Christine's father's car on one of his very first outings. Like Charlie of *Tirez sur le Pianiste,* he is sexually at ease only with a prostitute, and he is easily flustered by unexpected situations. In his first job as hotel clerk he is sent quickly into a panic by two men who burst in and demand to be taken to the room which the wife of one of them has rented. Antoine dashes frantically about trying to find the key, at last lets the men in, then turns away in shocked embarrassment as the naked woman rises indignantly from her bed and her lover scurries away desperately under the sheets. The husband sets about showing his displeasure by tearing up his wife's underclothing and smashing everything breakable in sight; the wife, breasts prominently in view, sits in the bed screaming furiously at him, and Antoine is caught between a surge of hilarity and his sense of modesty. The second man reveals himself as a private detective and suggests that Antoine 'phone the police; still flustered, he tries the fire brigade at first, and while he is talking his right hand is kept busy trying vainly to return a banknote which the detective constantly slips into it. In his later position as a private detective himself, Antoine hides behind a newspaper which he holds upside down and follows his prey with the inconspicuous grace of an elephant. Taken off trailing suspects, he is sent to work in M. Tabard's shoe shop, but first he has to compete for the job with several other applicants and parcel up a box of shoes better than any of them. The others do their work efficiently and neatly, while Antoine can't even get the wrapping to meet at either end, but as the job is fixed anyway he has to be proclaimed the winner.

Antoine finally stops hiding, comes into the open and accepts responsibility and maturity by proposing to Christine. At the same time, however, the mysterious stranger too "stops hiding"; he declares his love for Christine and tells her that he is "permanent" and will never betray her. The conjunction serves to undercut our wholehearted acceptance of the conventionally happy ending; though it does not by any means destroy it, it injects considerable ambiguity and, in combination with other scenes in the film, makes us wonder whether responsibility might not also mean stagnation and just how permanent "for ever" will be. The autumnal mood of this last scene, the grass a vivid green while the trees around are almost bare, is a perfect visual fusion of this ambiguity.*

The stranger and his motives are comic, pathetic and touching, and Truffaut's handling of other minor characters in the film confirms his insight into and compassion for the lonely, the outcast and the isolated. Most of these are created through gesture, tone of voice and facial expression as much as through dialogue—the homosexual who asks the detective agency to find his missing conjurer friend, and whose personality is perfectly created simply in the way in which he sits clasping one black-gloved hand and one bare one tightly in his lap; or M. Tabard, who talks about his problem of no one's liking him in a remote, detached tone of voice while he shifts uncomfortably in his seat. The only totally unsympathetic figure in the film is the woman in charge of Tabard's shoe shop, but she is so perfect an example of the "hatchet-faced" image that Truffaut can be forgiven his lapse from generosity here.

Antoine too is lonely; he is shy and clumsy both in physical activity and emotional relationships, although he carries through

*Though this film was actually made in early spring, the mood conveyed throughout is that of autumn.

his blunders with an engaging vitality and confidence which make it impossible for us to patronise him. He too is often most vividly created through gesture and movement, particularly in the two scenes in 'phone-booths where he extricates himself or others from difficult situations through quick thinking and action —qualities he is unable to emulate as successfully in face-to-face relationships. He can also behave with a certain panache when his only audience is himself—standing before his mirror chanting in succession the names "Christine Darbon," "Fabienne Tabard" and "Antoine Doinel" accompanied by intensely emotional hand movements, and finally dousing his face in cold water when the problem of choice becomes too much for him. Yet though he is in love with Christine, he doesn't quite know how to approach her; he tries to gain confidence with prostitutes, and then finds himself trapped into a brief and at first reluctant affair with Mme. Tabard instead.

Visual parallels between various types of sexual relationships throughout the film reflect Antoine's difficulties in adopting the right kind of approach to the right girl. In the brothel he attempts clumsily and almost brutally to kiss his partner as soon as they are alone together; when he and Christine go down to the cellar to collect some wine for dinner he tries suddenly to kiss her in exactly the same way. Both girls push him away, but the prostitute is still ready to offer her body while Christine is genuinely surprised and hurt. When Mme. Tabard finds her way to Antoine's room in the early morning he tries to hide under the bedclothes in the same gesture as that of the startled lover in the hotel scene earlier in the film. Mme. Tabard talks her way into bed with him, but it is typical of Truffaut's subtlety and honesty that a photo of Christine on Antoine's wall is unobtrusively brought into view during this scene. When Antoine, fortified by his experience with Mme. Tabard, at last finds the right method of approach for Christine, the camera tracks

*BAISERS VOLES: Antoine begins his incantation in the mirror*

from the discarded television set Antoine had come to repair, follows a trail of television innards across the room, moves slowly upstairs, looks briefly into Christine's empty bedroom, goes up more stairs, spots an empty slipper, and takes us into her parents' bedroom to glimpse the two lovers together before a swift and beautifully chaste fade-out—the whole paralleling the series of tracks and pans with which the camera follows the progress of Antoine's earlier letter to Mme. Tabard as it is carried through the pipes of the underground delivery system. It is through visual movement, gesture, setting, and repetition of this kind that Truffaut really tells us all we need to know about his characters.

Film by its very nature enables us to come to a fuller understanding of all the non-verbal clues to human behaviour and motives that psychiatrists and sociologists like Goffman[21] and Hall[22] have only quite recently begun to analyse in depth. (Many great novelists such as Dickens have been equally well aware of them, but words are a relatively clumsy and inexact way of coming to terms with something which can really only be reproduced visually.) Truffaut is more sensitive than most film directors to the ways in which the places we live in, both on the level of the city and the home, shape and condition the

*LA MARIEE ETAIT EN NOIR: Julie, Coral (Michel Bouquet) and phallic tiger-flowers. Blue and white patterned curtain in the background*

kinds of lives we lead. He is also aware that we reveal an immense amount about ourselves simply by the way we choose to respond to the limitations or potential that places offer us; we can surrender to them, adapting our personalities to suit the environment, as Pierre Lachenay or Charlie Koller do, or we can put up a fight as Antoine Doinel does. Our clothes, gestures, involuntary movements and habits of speech are not merely conscious or unconscious revelations of our own personality; they are constantly signalling our intentions towards other people and others misread them or ignore them at their peril. The objects with which we surround or decorate ourselves, the ways in which we choose to arrange the space around us, the distances at which we position ourselves from other people or objects are all clues to our attitudes and relationships, but even more, as they become habitual and instinctive they come to confine and control them. By showing us these things, with such insight, accuracy and humour, Truffaut again helps us towards freedom —the freedom to move away from constricting and unthinking patterns of behaviour, and realise more fully our own potential, the freedom too to understand what other people are *really* saying underneath all these words. He is also very conscious of the ways in which, like Pierre Lachenay or Julie Kohler, we are constantly playing roles, shifting the *façade* we present to the world according to the impression we wish to make and the audience we wish to impress, trying constantly to manipulate others even when least conscious that we are doing so. His films, through the subtle visual patterns and associations they set up, and through the accuracy and sympathy with which he observes and recreates so many aspects of human behaviour and the physical world with which we have surrounded ourselves, help to reveal to us more clearly our potential and our limitations and how to understand and work with both more effectively and humanely.

# 3. Voices and Reverberations

MUSIC IN MOST FILMS is either the equivalent of what semanticists call "phatic communion" or "verbal noise" (purely conventional or ritual sounds intended to fill in gaps or to prevent one from actually thinking about what one is saying), or it becomes blatant emotional manipulation, designed to do work that the director is too lazy or too inept to accomplish through visual effects or dialogue. Reacting against this, many important contemporary directors, such as Bergman, Bresson and Antonioni, have attempted to divest their films almost entirely of background music and have turned their attention instead to the blending of purely physical natural sounds, verbal nuances and intonations, and silence into an aesthetic harmony. Truffaut has no equivalent of the subtle orchestration of sound effects in *Shame* or *Mouchette*; like Resnais and Losey and some of the young Italian directors (Bertolucci, Bellocchio and Semperi) he aims for a blend of music and visuals throughout the film, the one reinforcing and commenting on the other. And like these directors he has no time for the conventional wisdom that the best film music is completely unobtrusive; in Truffaut's films the music becomes a vital, and noticeable, part of the total rhythm. It makes an essential contribution to the emotional effect, not by substituting for the visuals but by subtly interacting with them, creating a total structure in which both are integral elements. He very seldom uses music as a mere background accompaniment to dialogue, preferring anything up to half a dozen strongly melodic themes that are linked to particular characters, emotions or settings throughout. In recent films like *Fahrenheit 451*, *La Mariée Etait en Noir* and *Baisers Volés*, only one or two themes are developed consistently, the others being reduced to motifs of a few bars apiece, serving

110

as a kind of rhythmic continuity over the visual transitions or as brief definitions or reminders of a particular situation or character. When music is used, it can often be as important in shaking us out of conventional modes of response as some of the visual effects and transitions; this can also be achieved by the deliberate decision *not* to use music when the situation would seem to demand it—at moments of heightened tension or emotional power, or to accompany activity and movement. Almost the only conventional use of music in Truffaut's films, in fact, is to accompany and heighten moments of suspense—a legacy no doubt from Hitchcock, whose usual composer, Bernard Herrmann, he employed for *Fahrenheit 451* and *La Mariée Etait en Noir.*

Much of the lyrical effect of the films comes from the sheer sweep and flow of the music. This is most obviously true of *Jules et Jim,* yet much of this film is anticipated in the opening shots of *Les Mistons* where camera and music soar in unison with Bernadette as she cycles through the dazzling sunlight of the Provençal countryside. The surging and seemingly non-stop vitality of the music (substantially variations of two or three main themes, scored mainly for brass and woodwind) of the prewar scenes of *Jules et Jim* helps to involve us so completely in the rhythm and movement of the film that we have neither time nor inclination to pass judgement on the characters. Often camera, situation, action and music blend into a perfect harmony, as with Thérèse doing her steam-engine act in Jules's room or with the squeaky, jerky, sprightly tune that accompanies the sequence in which Catherine dresses up as a man. The music has an authentic period flavour throughout, intensified by the way in which the extracts from newsreels of the time are accompanied by the kind of tinkling piano music we associate with silent films (a device also prefigured in *Les Mistons* in the short re-creation of an early Lumière film). But there is not always this one-to-one relationship between music and visuals: in many cases the music is allowed to carry the main emotional effect while the images create the kind of not particularly lyrical everyday activity which gives the characters their naturalness and reality and without which all the joyous music in the world would not make them believable. This is particularly true of some of the opening scenes and of the holiday at the seaside, and the fusion of the two elements that results is essential for the success of the film: the music involves us with the characters while the images help us to believe in them. The two elements become interdependent, in much the same way as the flow and coherence of the music gives continuity to what might otherwise appear an abrupt and confusing succession of images.

The music, like the characters and the action, becomes more subdued in the second half of the film, where the two most characteristic themes are the sad and subdued "Fog" music and the bittersweet of Catherine's song "Le Tourbillon," which comes to take on more and more importance and is finally dominant as the film ends. With the music no longer a central and pervasive force in our consciousness, we are allowed, like the characters, to consider more closely the implications and consequences of a life that makes up its own rules as it goes along. Earlier themes are re-introduced in moments of happiness and reconciliation and sometimes accompany conversations such as that between Jim and Catherine on their walk through the woods at night, but they appear now as interludes rather than something integral to the characters' experience. Purely functional music associated with crisis and suspense and with little relation to the thematic structures of the rest of the film enters towards the end—successfully in the climactic scene of the death

*Opposite: in JULES ET JIM, Catherine cheats, but wins the race across the bridge (above), and prepares to jump into the Seine as Jules and Jim argue about women (below)*

of Jim and Catherine, less so in the melodrama of Catherine's earlier threat to shoot him. Truffaut, however, often creates moments of tension less conventionally and more convincingly by withdrawing the expected musical conditioning: the race across the bridge is silent except for the sounds of Catherine panting and the men gasping to catch up; her jump into the Seine, once the crisis point is reached, is also filmed with natural sound alone; and the beautiful and moving reconciliation between Catherine and Jules at the chalet, by omitting background music, achieves a dimension of painful honesty as the lovers try to drag words out of the silence to express themselves. And one of the most disturbing and enlightening moments of the film juxtaposes Catherine's pouring her vitriol down the sink with the soft lilt of the main love theme.

The music in *Jules et Jim* is among the most original and the most necessary ever written for any film. Without the music to evoke mood and atmosphere, to blend with or counterpoint the emotional impact of the visual images, to provide both the sense of a particular time and place *and* a continuity which spans a period of some twenty years in the structure of the film, and to engage the responses of the audience directly and forcefully from the very beginning, the difficulties presented by an episodic and disjointed story and characters removed to a large extent from conventional concerns and behaviour would probably have been insuperable. To say this is by no means to disparage Truffaut's visual sense or the way in which he skilfully condenses and rearranges the material of the original novel[18] (while remaining extremely faithful to it) to create something both coherent and complex, but rather to credit him with unusual intelligence and sensitivity in making full use of an element of the cinematic experience too often squandered or ignored.

It is not perhaps an accidental pattern that Truffaut so far has used each composer only for two consecutive films and then moved to someone else—Jean Constantin for *Les 400 Coups* and *Tirez sur le Pianiste*, Bernard Herrmann for *Fahrenheit 451* and *La Mariée Etait en Noir*, and Georges Delerue for *Jules et Jim* and *La Peau Douce*. The music, like the visual style of each film, has to be modified to suit the particular circumstances and requirements, but a composer may either consciously or unconsciously attempt to impose his personal style on all the films he writes for, or, having found a successful formula, he may attempt to reproduce this time after time. The latter certainly seems to have happened to Georges Delerue: after *Jules et Jim* he used virtually the same score for Ken Russell's *French Dressing*, and in *La Peau Douce* the love theme in particular is constantly

*LA PEAU DOUCE: Pierre (Jean Desailly) with Nicole in the motel*

reminiscent of the earlier film, though it is used with ironic subtlety and grace in its new setting. It first appears behind the credits as we see hands stroking and caressing each other; as we do not yet know who the lovers are, the theme takes on a certain impersonality or at least potentiality—it is waiting, so to speak, for someone to come along and claim it. It is briefly introduced as Nicole and Pierre meet in the lobby of the Lisbon hotel and pause momentarily to glance at each other and from then on it is constantly associated with the progress of their affair, most notably and beautifully in their first love scene, filmed, like that where Catherine and Jim first acknowledge their love for each other, without words, the camera concentrating on their faces caught in profile in the semi-darkness, and on their hands. But just as we have begun comfortably to associate Pierre-Nicole-love music we have the meeting of Pierre and Franca at the airport on his return, where the same theme is used to characterise their relationship, and we are subtly made aware that things are not going to be quite as simple as Pierre imagines. Pierre, like the music, has been waiting around for someone to claim him; he has neither the time nor the decisiveness to make the choice for himself. He proceeds to drift aimlessly from Nicole to Franca and back again, the music ironically accompanying him, playing its part impartially for Pierre and Nicole as they search around Paris to find a hotel for the night and for Pierre and Franca as they finally separate and Franca collapses in misery on to the sofa. Throughout the film the theme is sad and elegiac, even at the moments when the lovers come nearest to complete harmony, reflecting both the impossibility of the situation and our growing realisation that there is no satisfactory way out of it. Finally Nicole leaves, the music drifting around Pierre as he watches her from the half-finished apartment he had intended as their home, but the relationship with Franca has still to work itself out. Pierre assumes that they will find their way back together; he returns to his daily routine and waits for fate to step in and decide things for him. The music begins its final ironic metamorphosis, the love theme for Pierre as he sits at lunch in his restaurant being intercut with conventional suspense music as we see Franca on her way to shoot him. And after the killing we see her huddled in a corner, drained of passion, fear and satisfaction, and hear the love theme for the last time, now with its full implications of pain, misery, lost opportunities, tenderness and regret.

Elsewhere in the film music is used to reflect the chaos and fragmentation of the world the characters move in. The choppy vitality of the music that accompanies Pierre's desperate dashes to the airport, first to catch his 'plane to Lisbon and later to try to see Nicole before she leaves, captures the mood of anxiety and frustration, while that which accompanies his attempts to escape from his companion in Reims and return to the hotel has something of both the pathos and the ridiculousness of the situation in it. Though it is less original and less pervasive than in *Jules et Jim,* the music performs something of the same function in helping us adjust to the unusual rhythms of the visual style and, with the love theme in particular, making us uneasily aware of the tensions and complexities beneath an apparently straightforward surface.

In *Les 400 Coups* the music is more direct and less ambiguous. There are three or four main themes; each could be given a loose label such as "happiness," "escape," "sadness" and so on, and each is used as a direct reflection of the emotions conveyed by the visual images, rarely if ever undercutting or counterpointing them as in other films. Each scene of the film tends to form a self-contained whole, and although the recurrence of the basic themes is a force for continuity in the total pattern, the music itself seldom bridges the gap between scenes (one main exception being the overlapping of the music that accompanies Antoine on his way from the police station to jail. We are brought into close intimacy with Antoine in the police van through close-ups and through seeing the familiar streets as he now sees them, then we are abruptly removed from him and see only the bare walls and corridors as he is hustled to his cell—the continuity of the music helping to keep the emotional framework consistent). The very straightforwardness of the music is appropriate to the style of the film as a whole, which demands a direct response to facts and situations created with little regard for virtuosity or sophistication. The moods of the music directly reflect those of Antoine, thus heightening our involvement with him, and the fusion of Antoine, audience, music, sound, visuals and emotional effect is complete in the final shots as Antoine turns to gaze at the camera and the melodic unity breaks down into soft *pizzicato* and blends with the surging of the sea.

Almost the only noticeable use of music to counterpoint the visual images in this film comes as the sound of the "Marseillaise" on a neighboring radio swells out to accompany the sight of Antoine taking the garbage downstairs and scraping the oozing rubbish out of the can with his fingers—and here of course, as in the ironic tilt of the camera to take in "Liberté, Egalité, Fraternité" as the children pour out of the gates of their school/prison, the effect is to align us unambiguously with Antoine against the false pretensions and claims of his society. And as in the other films the music is used only where it is *needed:* dialogue is generally presented without background accompaniment and in scenes where music would be purely conventional (the stealing of the typewriter, for example) it is usually omitted.

Though I personally find the music of *Les 400 Coups* satisfactory in its creation of a sense of lyricism in the grubby back

118

streets of Paris and its involvement of the audience in Antoine's experiences, it is possible for an unsympathetic viewer to find it closer to the traditional emotional conditioning of the audience than that of any other of Truffaut's films. Jean Constantin's music for *Tirez sur le Pianiste,* however, is required to serve totally different purposes and the result is a score almost as subtle and as essential to the final impact of the film as that of *Jules et Jim.* Much of the sound in the film is "natural," in the sense that it consists of music played by Charlie as part of his daily work (this device is used also in *L'Amour à Vingt Ans* where virtually all the music consists of the classical music Antoine hears at concerts, plays in the record shop he works in, or listens to on his record-player). Charlie is identified from the beginning with one particular tune, one he knows so well that he can play it without thinking, just as he tries to lead a life so centred round routine and mechanical repetition of the same experiences that he will no longer need to think or feel about anything. In the scenes in the bar at the beginning of the film we see other ways in which music can be used to deaden, avoid or smooth over unexpected emotional eruptions. After the fracas with the gangsters and their pursuit of Chico the waiter's song immediately establishes order and routine and the customers forget the incident at once, while throughout these scenes the incessant slickness of the dance music provides a background to an astonishing variety of sexual advances—which, because of the background, are taken for granted and unresented.

The first "unnatural" music in the film establishes the basic love theme as Charlie and Lena walk home from the bar, but background music as such is relatively sparse. The love theme, generally restrained and subdued like that of *La Peau Douce,* undergoes the same kind of process as the closing music of *Les 400 Coups,* rising to a note of anguished finality and abruptness as the camera zooms in on Lena's face as she lies dead in the

*TIREZ SUR LE PIANISTE: Charlie at his piano, in the bar . . .*

snow. Elsewhere music is used for scenes of violent activity like Charlie's fight with the barman and the final shoot-out at the farm, for moments of suspense and waiting, to cover transitions, and in the major love scenes—with Clarisse, the sound of a radio from next door (suggesting perhaps the mechanical nature of the relationship); with Theresa, "their" love theme; with Lena, Charlie's piano tune orchestrated so that it is both different and recognisable, just as his love for Lena has only superficially affected his general outlook on life. But the main originality of the music rests in the way in which the virtual identity of Charlie and his piano is conveyed throughout. The flashback to his days as a concert pianist is introduced by the normal piano theme modulating into a piece of classical music; it ends with

*. . . and in the concert hall*

Charlie's circling round the piano in the bar, sitting down and striking a few resounding concert-like blows while a dissolve covers an almost automatic and inevitable drift into the tune that is to provide his identity, his shell and his armour for the rest of his life. Later,. as Lena and the barman quarrel, he wanders over to the piano and tinkles a few notes on it before making his one belated and disastrous attempt to become involved with something outside himself. And at the end he briefly tries out a new tune before slipping, unconsciously and inexorably, into the routine he can never again escape from.*

*Some North American prints of the film crudely overemphasise Charlie's impasse by a voice-over repetition here of the barman's earlier "Music is what we need, man!" which is not in the original French prints.

In *Les Mistons* and his first four features Truffaut generally uses music thematically—to define characters and situations, to create atmosphere and mood, and to provide juxtapositions and ironies which add an extra dimension to the surface action of visuals and dialogue. In the next three features music plays a less obvious but still important role and its function could perhaps be best described as a rhythmic one, creating a sense of flow and continuity in what are often very episodic structures. There is still an association of particular themes with characters, moods and situations, but these tend to be presented in a kind of shorthand way and are rarely developed as extensively or as richly as in the earlier films. *Baisers Volés* (with

*BAISERS VOLES: Antoine makes advances to Christine (Claude Jade) in the wine cellar . . .*

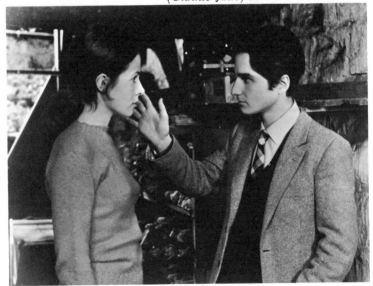

music this time by Antoine Duhamel) is perhaps closest to the earlier style with its gently elegiac love theme turning up in brief snatches throughout the film (reflecting Antoine's inability to commit himself fully to an emotional relationship) and finally working itself out fully and leisurely as it accompanies the camera on its search from the sitting room upstairs to find Christine and Antoine in bed—with an exquisite moment of silence as the camera glances into the wrong bedroom on the way. The theme thus completes or finds itself in much the same way as Antoine does, but the relationship between music and character is not as intricate as in *Tirez sur le Pianiste* or *La Peau Douce*. Other themes are less developed and are used

*. . . and is rewarded*

mainly either as structural devices (the "activity" theme that accompanies Antoine on his way to bungle another assignment) or to inject a note of unease (the "follower" theme for the stranger trailing Christine) or simply to characterise figures such as Mme. Tabard. As in *Les 400 Coups* music is sometimes used to create an impression of violent movement while the camera remains relatively static—in the fights in the hotel bedroom and the agency office. As usual too, music is rarely placed behind dialogue, although it is very effectively used in the scene in which Antoine meets an old friend down on his luck, the music of the love theme contrasting ironically the circumstances of the two, and heightening Antoine's embarrassment at his inability to deal adequately with the situation. The lack of music, on the other hand, after the scene in which Antoine clumsily tries to kiss Christine in the cellar intensifies both the comedy and the pathos of the situation as the girl turns in silence and leaves, and Antoine after a moment follows. And in the scene of his seduction by Mme. Tabard the sound of her soft voice competing with the early morning traffic gives the situation an authenticity that music could only have spoiled.

Conversely, *Fahrenheit 451* often uses music behind dialogue in a way that is uncharacteristic of Truffaut and at times both distracting and annoying. The music in the love scene between Montag and Linda is obtrusive and unnecessary, detracting from whatever impact the scene might otherwise have, and that which accompanies Montag's reading from *David Copperfield* dangerously focuses on the sentimentality of Dickens's death-bed description rather than intensifying the dignity which it is presumably meant to have in this context. Music is most effectively used in this film as rhythmic enhancement of visual motion—the bursts of sound which accompany the monorail back and forth to the city and which help to give the scurrying fire-engine the toy-like effect that Truffaut says he aimed for.

This effect is picked up and used more extensively in *La Mariée Etait en Noir,* where music and camera flow together at the beginning of each episode as Julie tracks down and closes in on her victims, the rippling music contributing largely to the fluid, dance-like impression which the film as a whole creates. The insistent repetition and abrupt breaking-off of the wedding march, with its final completion as Julie comes to the end of her list of victims, achieves the same kind of definition of the character as the fragmentation and final harmonising of the love theme does in *Baisers Volés,* as well as serving as a structural centre for the film itself. *La Mariée* has its own love theme, though character and situation allow it little scope for development—it is heard mainly as a brief introduction to Bliss's party, during Julie's second visit to Fergus, as she poses for him as Diana and begins to be uneasily aware of her attraction towards him, and as Fergus desperately paints her picture on the wall above his bed after she leaves. And as Bernard Herrmann is also Hitchcock's composer for several recent films, there are, as in *Fahrenheit 451,* moments of instantly recognisable suspense music to draw our attention to significant actions such as Julie's pouring her glass of water into the flower-pot on Bliss's balcony (a gesture that has to be firmly fixed in our minds for us to be able to pick up its repetition later in the film).

Some of the most interesting aural effects in the film come from a dislocation between music, sound and image that is uncharacteristic of Truffaut but suits very well the atmosphere of strangeness, of things not quite fitting together in the right way, of this particular work. Julie's mandolin record is seen on the record-player as she poisons Coral's arak, but it is different music that we hear. In his room she puts the record on and dances for him, but half-way through the music changes to something which suits better the hallucinatory images that begin to appear. The flashback that re-creates the events of the shooting of her husband on their wedding day is conveyed very effectively with music only: the characters talk but we hear no dialogue and no natural sounds—except those of the rifle being loaded and fired. The scene has a dream-like, unreal quality (just as Julie's marriage is the fulfilment of her childhood dreams) which is irrevocably and unexpectedly shattered by the rifle. Julie's appearance at Fergus's funeral has a similar dream-like effect, created in much the same way through music and the denial to the audience of the words that are clearly being spoken, though this time there is a full background of natural sound.

If music plays a less dominant role in *La Mariée Etait en Noir* and *Baisers Volés* than in the earlier films, it is nevertheless equally integral to the total pattern, contributing immeasurably to the effect of rhythmic grace that these films convey, as well as providing crucial insights into character and establishing atmosphere and tone. The vital importance of music to the final effect of Truffaut's films can also be seen in his use of songs to give an extra dimension to people and actions.

The theme songs of *Baisers Volés,* with its emphasis on young love as something fugitive and quickly passing, establishes a tone of wistfulness and regret that provides an undercurrent to the comedy and happiness of much of the action and surfaces in the repetition of the song at the end to put our acceptance of the "happy-ever-after" ending into a new perspective. Catherine's song in *Jules et Jim* comes very near the middle of the film and provides both a commentary on the action to that point and a foretelling of the way the situation will develop. Its recurring pattern of meeting/brief affair/parting/being drawn together again is a summary of the action of the whole film, and its themes of the fascination exerted by the woman and the inability of the men ever to escape completely from her take on peculiar force when the music of the song closes the film and

Jules walks away in apparent freedom. At the same time the gaiety of the tune works together with the sombre implications of the words in much the same way as the style of the whole film achieves a perfect fusion of romance, wish-fulfilment, historical fact and psychological realism.

In *Tirez sur le Pianiste* the two songs heard in the bar at the beginning of the film both deal with sex as a crudely pleasurable physical activity in much the same way as most of the conversations and actions in the first half of the film do, and as Charlie would like to be able to and thus avoid the complications of giving himself emotionally. The second song in particular, with its breathless succession of apparent nonsense words (flashed out on the screen even in the French version to reassure audiences that they are hearing what they think they are) catches perfectly the tone and mood of the visual side of the film, with, in both cases, serious implications hidden underneath. Later in the film, the song Charlie and Lena hear on the car radio as they drive to the farm (the words continuous over a series of dissolves in space and time) takes up the themes of loyalty, betrayal and emotional honesty that are on the point of working themselves out. Though there are no songs as such in *La Mariée Etait en Noir* (apart from Robert Coral's pathetic and ironic little song of happiness after he has made a date with Julie), the recurrence of the mandolin record before the first three murders has almost the effect of a song, and the fact that we are never told why Julie plays this particular record or what it means to her adds to the aura of mystery and strangeness around her.

My inability to appreciate opera makes me hesitate to call Truffaut's films "operatic," but some such word is necessary to convey the complete interdependence of music, song, words, visual effects and setting in his films. Perhaps once again his own comment on his films as a kind of circus is helpful, for the

127

music plays a crucial role in creating the sense of vitality and variety, producing a complete range of emotional effects experienced either successively or simultaneously, and above all presenting a film as something to be *enjoyed* on as many levels of response, aural, visual, emotional and intellectual, as possible.

✣ ✣ ✣

The importance placed on music in Truffaut's films makes it inevitable that the orchestration of natural sounds should play a comparatively minor role. In films where music is sparse or non-existent a director can obtain immensely subtle effects from the sound of bird-song, the scrape of footsteps on gravel, the creak of a door opening or shutting, or the rustle of wind through grass and leaves. We rarely remember sounds of this kind from a Truffaut film—perhaps the creaking of the rocking chair in the chalet as Jules and Jim meet again for the first time since before the War and neither can think of anything to say, or the waves breaking on the shore at the end of *Les 400 Coups* or swamping Jules and Jim as Catherine impassively looks on, perhaps the blaring of the car horn as Catherine drives around the square outside Gilberte's apartment and succeeds in waking Jim, or the ticking of the clock as Charlie waits through the night in his brothers' shack—but these are relatively infrequent. Natural sounds are used for thematic effect chiefly in *Les 400 Coups* and *La Peau Douce*: in the former the harsh, grating noises of daily activity in the school room are echoed in both jail and reformatory, creating an atmosphere of aural bleakness from which Antoine seldom escapes (even the revolving drum at the fairground produces a mechanical, monotonous, inhuman sound), and in the latter the abrupt, peremptory sound of buzzers, doors clicking open and shut, cases being thrown into cars and luggage racks, gear changes, jet planes, incessant traffic all help to create the impersonal fragmented environment of the film.

A more important effect is that created simply by tone of voice, vocal emphasis or monotony and pace of speech in many of the films. The underlying tensions of the marriage between Jules and Catherine are forced to the surface, not by explicit dialogue, analysis or action, but by Catherine responding to Jules's harmless remark about Jim's fondness for German beer by a breathlessly passionate outpouring of the varieties and names of as many French wines as she can think of, unmistakably aligning herself with her countryman against Jules, who has suddenly become an intruder and a foreigner. Later in the film Thérèse's non-stop harangue to Jim listing her innumerable lovers since she last saw him (a discourse to which Jim pays virtually no attention) provides a wry commentary on the bed-swopping now well under way in the main love triangle. A similar effect occurs in *La Mariée Etait en Noir* as Clément Morane drones on and on about his professional shrewdness and ability to manipulate others for his own ends (stopping only to issue a perfunctory, "Don't forget to say your prayers," as Cookie goes off to bed) while the impassive Julie wanders about the kitchen looking for a suitable method of killing him.

Some of the most penetrating revelations into character and motive in the films come merely from the way in which words are spoken. In *Les 400 Coups* the sudden pleasure in Antoine's voice as he comes home to find his father alone and asks "Maman est partie?" (the implication being that he thinks she has left for good), and the mingled delight and desperation with which he rounds on his teacher and snarls that his mother is dead, are in themselves enough to illuminate completely his whole relationship with his mother. As Charlie prepares to leave the bar at the end of a day's work the barman starts a conversation (inevitably about sex and his own personal disappoint-

*JULES ET JIM: Jim meets
Thérèse on a trip to Paris*

ments) and tries some amateur psychoanalysis on Charlie, telling
him that he is timid. "J'ai peur . . . merde, j'ai peur . . . j'ai
peur," Charlie muses, almost as though he is trying out emotions
for size and this one had never occurred to him before.
Antoine's naïvety and enthusiasm in *Baisers Volés* emerge in
his constant self-dramatisation and consequent overdoing of
vocal effects—the strained volubility with which he tries to
convince a colleague of his sexual conquests, to which the other

replies with a far-fetched story of his own (ironically and literally turned hollow as the two men walk down the stairway to a *métro* station); the ecstatic admiration with which he describes Mme. Tabard to a fellow detective on the 'phone only to be wearily told to stick to the facts; and the self-induced frenzy with which he recites the series of names to his reflection in the mirror. The tone of Pierre's first 'phone call to Nicole in *La Peau Douce* catches perfectly his hesitation, self-doubt, subdued eagerness, embarrassment and confusion, as well as the mixture of regret and relief with which he receives her refusal (he had made an attempt and yet doesn't have to commit himself after all)—all the features, in fact, which will ensure that the affair is a complete disaster. A general flatness and deadness of expression is pervasive throughout *Fahrenheit 451*, often very effectively. The artificial and "personalised" warmth of the television announcer, the two homosexuals discussing flatly and mechanically how to arrange the seating at their party, then staring straight at the camera to ask accusingly, "What do you think, Linda?", the voices of Linda's friends as they talk in the same monotone of daily trivialities and the possibilities of their husbands' deaths in war, together with the fact that they can muster up little more emotion to express their horror at Montag's heresies, the dead voice of the neighbour who tells Montag that Linda has disappeared—all these convey very well the stifling, monotonous atmosphere of the society the film creates. The effect is somewhat undercut, however, when the same kind of deadness appears in the speech of Montag, Clarisse and all the book people at the end, for it implies that there is little more genuine vitality or spontaneity in their alternative than in what they are fighting against.

So much of the emotional and thematic impact of a Truffaut film is contained in camera movement, editing, facial expression, gesture, physical activity, setting, music and tone of voice that there would seem to be little need for dialogue, yet there is a good deal of talk in all the films. The dialogue is rarely, however, analytical or explanatory, the other aural and visual elements of the films having virtually eliminated the need for this; instead it consists largely of the ordinary, apparently "useless" speech that makes up a large proportion of everyday conversation and that unobtrusively conveys a great deal about the characters and their habitual, almost instinctive assumptions and responses, as well as contributing to the sense of naturalness and spontaneity so characteristic of the films. It seldom takes precedence over the visuals and there are few particularly memorable, witty or poetic lines (though some anecdotes and stories stick in the mind), but it is a vital and fully integrated element in the final concept.

Truffaut has worked on the script of all his films, though always in collaboration; occasionally the dialogue is credited to one of the other writers, but the same features are found to a greater or lesser extent throughout, adapted to suit the circumstances of each film. The pattern of Truffaut's own films appears even in a film which he did not direct but for which he worked on the scenario and wrote the dialogue—his friend Jean-Louis Richard's *Mata-Hari*. This is a film which owes an immense amount to *Jules et Jim,* particularly in the way in which the pre-Great War period setting is used and actual newsreel shots of the time are integrated into the period re-creation (some of the same War shots being used in both films). The dialogue is constantly low-keyed, refusing to emphasise or even pay much attention to the traditional dramatic potential of beautiful spies—ecstatic protestations of undying love, harangues about duty and patriotism, or confrontations between traitress and deluded lover. Instead attention is focused on the everyday exchanges and conversations that give the characters a welcome reality and humanity, more literary emotions being appropriately conveyed by letter, with a warmth and sensuality reminiscent of Jules's war letters to Catherine. The result is something like the tension between conventional filmic expectations and what we actually see on the screen that is created in *Tirez sur le Pianiste,* though much of this effect comes less from dialogue than from non-verbal situations whose inspiration can be attributed only to Truffaut—a spy desperately trying to steal a briefcase handcuffed to a chair is reduced to carrying off the chair itself and promptly falls down the stairs with it; on his way back to replace it after exchanging the contents his car breaks down and he is forced to travel by *métro.* Fleeing from the police after a confederate's arrest, Mata-Hari is followed by a suspicious looking man who turns out simply to be after a pick-up. Almost the only verbal exchange in the film equivalent to this is that where a vain and pompous officer asks Mata-Hari to guess his age and she promptly and unerringly replies "forty-six."

In *Les 400 Coups* and *Baisers Volés* the dialogue plays an essential part in reinforcing the sense of familiar and universal experience that makes these films so memorable. The rhythms, the awkwardness, the rituals, the trivialities and banalities of everyday verbal encounters are all caught with subtlety and lack of insistence. The characters are filled in through speech, the routine exchanges of school, family and office, rather than completely defined by them—it is their ability to escape from or transcend these routines that gives them their full humanity. In *Les 400 Coups* speech is relatively useless as a method of genuine communication and Antoine's attempts to explain himself in school, family and reformatory are constantly futile and lead only to incessant misunderstanding; language in this film centres round the small exchanges which create verisimilitude (Truffaut showing a particular gift for the coarseness and sheer loudness of children's speech here as in *Les Mistons*), or articulate antagonisms, or grope towards temporary reconciliation, or deaden sensitivity towards mind-numbing routines, while the visual element conveys the genuine emotions of happiness and misery. In *Baisers Volés* language has a rather more positive role: Antoine can at least talk freely and openly to Christine's parents, though what he actually *says* rarely goes beyond the conventional noises expressing goodwill. He is in fact constantly talking, bubbling over with enthusiasm and a desire to impress, eliciting from other people either amused liking (Christine's parents), tolerant indifference (most of the other characters) or exasperated antagonism (the manageress of the shoe shop and, finally, his boss at the detective agency). Both his words themselves and his inability to be silenced except by an emotional crisis convey his fundamental insecurity and immaturity and also the genuine spontaneity and integrity underneath. Christine on the other hand is relatively silent throughout, she deliberately keeps herself aloof and enigmatic, melting just often enough to let Antoine know she is still available and to encourage him to keep trying. His obtuseness exasperates her, while her alternations between warmth and coolness puzzle him; their conversations tend therefore to be tense and unsatisfactory, breaking out occasionally into open hostility. They communicate much better in silence, through smiles and touches, and his proposal is appropriately carried out in writing and dumb-show. Almost all the important actions and relationships in the film complete themselves outside the dialogue, yet without Truffaut's sensitivity to the way in which people attempt at least to express themselves through words the film would lose much of its intimacy and credibility. Some of the background exchanges in particular, consisting often of a few hesitant or angry words (such as the woman detective's sudden resentment of a colleague's insistent advances, or Antoine's meeting with a former girl friend—Colette of *L'Amour à Vingt Ans*) give the film a dimension and an honesty that would elude a more "sophisticated" or "literary" concept of dialogue.

Speech can often be a form of self-definition, valuable more to the speaker than to the person addressed (who is usually not listening in any case). Many of the conversations in Truffaut's films are virtual monologues, the characters arguing with or explaining themselves rather than making any real attempt to complete a dialogue. Antoine tries to explain his love of Balzac to his mother; she responds by talking about the importance of getting on in life and then launches into a totally irrelevant account of her childhood love-life while her bored son leans on his elbow and gazes dispassionately into the distance. With the psychiatrist he answers a series of purely routine questions, attempting to define himself and his behaviour as honestly as possible, but the questioner, like society as a whole, is not really concerned with him or what he needs, and once her duty has been done in asking the questions she shows no interest or even surprise at the answers.

This quality of conversation as monologue is strongest, and thematically most appropriate, in *La Peau Douce* and *La Mariée Etait en Noir*. Pierre and Nicole cannot really get together on any level, physical, emotional or intellectual. Pierre carries his everyday business attitudes and habits over into his love relationships, he tends to lecture Nicole most of the time, talking *at* her rather than *to* her. Catching himself doing this, he then slips to the opposite extreme and becomes hesitant, indecisive and apologetic. His inability to strike the right balance in his love relationships contrasts markedly to his self-assurance in the lecture-hall setting where he knows exactly what is expected of him and what the response is likely to be. He takes his wife Franca for granted, rarely speaking to her except on conventional household matters or to quarrel. She constantly tries to get through to him, but he is usually too busy or too pre-

*LA PEAU DOUCE: Franca (Nelli Bénédetti) pleads with Pierre*

occupied with other matters to listen. Nicole is equally self-absorbed; she speaks very little, but when she does it is usually to talk either about herself or about sex. The impasse between the three people is complete: Franca wants to communicate, but Pierre refuses to listen to her. He in turn tries to make contact with Nicole but fails because he knows only two languages—that of self-projection through professional achievement and that of apologetic self-doubt and self-examination, neither of them suited to a girl with a taste for glamour and emotional excitement. And Nicole is too wrapped up in her own concerns to even make the attempt to adjust to what little Pierre has to offer her. The most articulate character in the film, Clément, Pierre's acquaintance in Reims, is also ironically the most boring, and he too spends most of his time talking to himself. Yet though words prove incapable of closing the gaps between people and the characters are reduced ultimately to basic physical gestures to get their point across—Nicole turning and walking out of Pierre's life and Franca driven to killing him—the actual dialogue of the film communicates the hesitations, the misunderstandings and the barriers with vividness and truth.

Julie Kohler's concern to present an enigmatic, impenetrable *façade* results in her remaining silent and mysterious in most of her encounters with her victims. She talks little, mostly in terms of hints and suggestions which the others are quick to seize on and interpret and elaborate to their own satisfaction. She is most articulate when recalling to Morane the circumstances of the murder, but her version of the story has obviously become so obsessional with her that his explanation of how the shooting *really* occurred makes no impression whatever, and she continues with her plan as though nothing had changed. Julie carries to an extreme the tendency not to listen to or be affected by the attempts of other people to communicate, just as she refuses to pay attention to the alternatives in the physical and moral world around her, but most of the men she encounters do little better. Their conversation gives them a vivid concrete reality (a remarkable achievement considering how short a role each of them plays) yet at the same time it is curiously introverted. Bliss, polished, elegant, superficial, muses constantly on his past sexual conquests and his future potential. Robert Coral, pathetically insecure, keeps up a steady stream of noise to himself even when alone (disbelievingly accepting a letter addressed to him he mutters, "Monsieur Coral, c'est moi," with an air of surprise, as though recognising his identity for the first time), and even when Julie is in his room his words are less

directed to her than an attempt to convince himself that all this is really happening to him. Clément Morane talks solely to impress, to project an image of himself and is so pleased with the result that it doesn't matter to him whether others are listening or not. The brutish Delvaux is almost completely inarticulate, while Fergus tends constantly to pose, presenting like Morane an image of himself, but sensitive enough to realise when it has become inadequate. In particular he is acutely self-conscious about the sexual impact he is making and, like many self-proclaimed libertines, experiences a curious compulsion to convince others verbally of his prowess. The concern of all of them to project or study themselves rather than to attempt to understand Julie leads of course to disaster.

It is only in *Fahrenheit 451* that Truffaut abandons this concern with "useless" dialogue, with allowing characters either to reveal themselves unconsciously through their everyday speech habits or to make a conscious or semi-conscious attempt to impose their idealised self-image on others. There are few of the asides, the casual remarks, the spontaneous interludes that give depth and authenticity to the other films; instead there are not only the long explanatory speeches of the Captain, Clarisse and others, but even minor exchanges are fraught with meaning and significance. One reason for this seems to be Truffaut's desire to keep the essence of the film close to that of the book: though characters are fused together, changed or invented (in particular the figure of Clarisse) and incidents are often altered or re-modelled, almost every word of the film has its counterpart somewhere in Bradbury's novel, and even verbal images like Mildred's (the name of the wife in the novel) association of books with vermin or the comparison of the

*Opposite: Oskar Werner (left) and Truffaut in the snow for the last scene of FAHRENHEIT 451*

helicopters searching for Montag to "the first flakes of snow in the long winter to come" are given a visual counterpart in the film, even if in a different context.* But by taking over the language of the novel, Truffaut unfortunately inherits its portentousness as well.

*Jules et Jim* is also very close in tone and language to its original—a novel by Henri-Pierre Roché[18]—but here the source is much closer in spirit and outlook to Truffaut's own and his respect for it does not have the effect of stifling some of his basic creative impulses. Many of the incidents in the book are compressed, omitted or re-arranged (for the better—the novel becomes excessively diffuse and fragmented in space and time towards the end and Truffaut tightens it up to good effect), and the characters too are reduced to manageable numbers (Catherine is given some of the characteristics and actions of some of Jules's German girl friends in the novel as well as those of the original Kate), but the pattern and in particular the language of the book remain much the same. Truffaut, however, gives his film, through the use of music and camera movement, a lyrical sweep and dimension which the book, essentially impersonal and objective, lacks, and he also infuses a sympathy and involvement with the characters which Roché seems deliberately to avoid. The result is one of the most remarkable adaptations in the history of the cinema, a work which in its main themes, its arrangement of incident and detail, and its conception of character remains very faithful to its original, and yet, while inventing and adding virtually nothing in terms of action, results in something completely unique and individual and impossible to think of as anything other than a film.

*Though the episode with the book people was not originally intended as a snow scene, the accident of snow falling during shooting was intelligently exploited to crystallise the already implicit idea of the "long winter" ahead of them.

Truffaut retains much of Roché's objectivity in the dialogue of the film and, like him, makes little attempt to explain or justify the characters psychologically. In the prewar scenes the dialogue departs most radically from the novel, and consists mainly of the kind of everyday exchanges which give the characters the familiarity and naturalness that Roché's ultimately lack. Where conversations from the novel are introduced, they are often given an unexpected twist: a German girl called Gertrud tells in the book the story of her dream of meeting Napoleon in a lift, his getting her with child and leaving her; it is Truffaut's Catherine telling the story who adds the revealing "Poor Napoleon!" The dialogue reflects the carefree, spontaneous, uncomplicated existence which the trio are leading at this point; they behave instinctively, refusing to analyse either themselves or the consequences of their actions. The visuals and the music carry most of the "meaning" of the film at this stage, while the words help us to accustom ourselves to and accept the characters. After the War the pace of the film slows down, conversations become longer and more explicit as the characters come painfully to terms with the complexity of personal relationships and are forced to try to analyse their own and others' motives. There is more introspection and self-analysis, more argument and explanation, much of it taken directly from the book and slightly more stylised than the dialogue earlier in the film (for example, Jim's speech to Catherine on page ninety-seven of the English version of the script).[2] The stylisation, however, seems appropriate to the belated attempt at understanding that is taking place.

The characters nevertheless are not equipped to understand themselves or each other fully and Truffaut uses Roché's narrator to bring out the implications which they are incapable of reaching on their own. The narrator speaks something like a third of the words actually heard in the film and provides an element of continuity and consistency throughout. His tone is one of detachment and objectivity: he will explain thoughts (those of Jim waiting for Catherine in the café), articulate emotions which the characters are unable or unwilling to follow through for themselves (those of all three after Catherine's leap into the Seine), analyse character (Catherine in some of the scenes at the chalet), occasionally speak for them (summing up Jim's side of his conversation with Catherine on their night walk), give factual information (during the War scenes), or provide a final summing-up at the end of the film, but he is never moralistic and never passes value judgements. The criticism that the use of a narrator is "uncinematic" is worthless when faced with its triumphant success *as* cinema in this case. Not only does the narrator play a valuable structural role in the compression and continuity of a great variety of incidents, he gives the remainder of the film (dialogue, visuals and music) an independence which they could never have had if they had been forced to substitute for him as well. The result is the added dimension which avoids the aura of slightly clinical coldness that surrounds the novel and allows Truffaut to achieve a combination of objectivity, honesty and involvement and yet leave both characters and audience with freedom and independence.

Truffaut has used a narrator in two other films, *Les Mistons* and *L'Amour à Vingt Ans*. In the former the retrospective irony of the narrator places both the crudeness and the innocence of the young boys into perspective, allowing us to share with him both the genuine charm and freedom of a particular stage of childhood and the inevitable awakening to experience which must follow. In the latter there is again a distancing effect as we re-live with Antoine the disappointments and brief happiness of young love, yet realise too that this is merely a stage which everyone has to pass through—but the same sort of effect is achieved without a narrator in *Baisers Volés* and the main reason for using one may simply be economy in attempting to create, develop and end a relationship in twenty-five minutes of film.

Charlie Koller's series of interior monologues in *Tirez sur le Pianiste* has something of the effect of a narrator explaining his thoughts, but it is really much closer to the kind of incessant inner conversation that we all carry on with ourselves almost every waking minute. It expresses very forcefully the essential conflict between the two aspects of Charlie's personality, summing up his fears, hopes, regrets, desires and good intentions, together with his inability to do anything about them at the right time. He is constantly addressing himself in questions or imperatives, asking what he should do or desperately trying to order himself into action. There is only one occasion where the promptings of his inner voice and his actual behaviour coincide: after Chico has fled from the bar pursued by the gangsters, Charlie tells himself not to get involved and simply "say good luck to him," following this with a muttered "Bonne chance!" aloud. But where the inner voice recommends involvement Charlie does his best not to listen and, if he does act, does so half-heartedly and too late. The result is not always as tragic as when he tells himself to forgive and comfort his wife when she confesses her infidelity, but yields instead to jealousy and inertia, leaves, changes his mind and returns to find her dead. Walking along the street with Lena he holds an anguished debate as to whether to try to hold her hand, attempts fumblingly to do so and is repulsed, then rehearses various elegant and sophisticated ways of asking her to have a drink with him before blurting out "D'ya want a drink?" only to find that she has vanished (a scene that reminds me irresistibly of Charlie Brown trying to think of the right words with which to present his Valentine to the little red-haired girl and doing so finally with a confident "Happy Christmas!" Both Charlies possess a common inability to make their inner and outer worlds coincide or even come within touching distance). The final metamorphosis of the inner voice ironically reverses the normal process as Charlie sits at his piano during the quarrel in the bar telling himself to stay out of it and suddenly finds himself taking part after all.

The dualities of Charlie's nature and of the world he moves in are echoed in the dialogue elsewhere in the film. The language of most of the characters is extremely slangy, down-to-earth, full of sexual jokes and innuendoes, reflecting Charlie's desire to punish himself by forcing himself into as sordid an environment as he can stand and systematically debasing or ignoring the values he had lived by previously. Conversations are short and terse, and Charlie himself speaks as little and as briefly as possible. He chooses to be in this environment but can never be fully part of it, as we see in the conversation in the car with the gangsters where Lena's smile becomes more and more knowing as the coarseness of the conversation becomes more explicit, till she finally takes an active part in it, while Charlie sits rather bewildered in the back seat and finally ventures as his contribution his father's remark that once you've seen one woman you've seen them all. The characters of this milieu are constantly attempting to explain and define themselves, but have neither the verbal nor the intellectual sophistication to succeed, though their very attempts are enough to give us insight into them. The flashback shows us a different world, where people talk more fluently and coherently, but where Charlie is equally ill at ease and uncomfortable. He can adjust fully to neither world, verbally, emotionally or morally, and the result is the insecurity which plagues him throughout.

Truffaut catches in almost every film the unpretentious, normal, colloquial vocabulary and rhythms which root his people firmly in a real time and place, and give them both individuality and relevance to their context. More than this, he shows how we use or misuse words to hinder rather than achieve communication, preferring to dramatise our own personal worlds and concerns rather than opening both them and ourselves to the attention, and possibly the assistance, of others.

*Truffaut directing Jean-Pierre Cargol in L'ENFANT SAUVAGE*

# 4. Dream and Reality

You ask me what it is that I do
when I dream? I will tell you
what you do when you are awake.
You take me, the me of dreams, me
the totality of your past, and you
force me, by making me smaller and
smaller, to fit into the little
circle that you trace around your
present action.
(Henri Bergson, *Dreams*)

IN ITS SUSPENSION of our normal conscious concerns and everyday reactions, the cinema is very close to the dream. In the dream world of the cinema we respond to wishes, behaviour, actions which heighten, distort or transform those of ordinary experience. Film can set aside the logical process and take us into a world where our deepest desires and fears are fulfilled (two recent films in which the dreams of characters and audience are inextricably blended are *Shame* and *Point Blank*).

The atmosphere of Truffaut's films is rarely explicitly dream-like (exceptions are parts of *Jules et Jim* and *La Mariée Etait en Noir*), but the process which takes place in them is similar to that of the dream. In dreams we find our own natures and those of other people changed, we find ourselves doing things we would seldom "dream of" in waking life. Our personalities undergo subtle shifts, as do those of people we encounter, resulting in a mixture of familiarity and strangeness, often bringing to light aspects of character and behaviour more true and reliable than those of conscious assessments. In Truffaut's films style, setting, rhythm and music carry out the function of dream displacement and conventional responses are given no chance to take over; the world we experience is basically familiar but presented in a way which removes false recognition and security, the standardised, unthinking assumptions of everyday life. People and actions are recognisable, yet set in combinations and associations which expose us to new experiences and demand fresh responses. The result is to make us return to the world outside the cinema with the kind of insight into ourselves and other human beings that we could gain from dreams if pressures from within and outside ourselves did not quickly combine to make us forget or reject the dream-knowledge. The impact of the film is not shrugged off so easily, however, and should have the effect of freeing us, for a time at least, from our normal inhibitions and prejudices and allowing us to act and think with a new freedom from the lazy or selfish assumptions we normally let ourselves be guided by. We move outside the "little circle" of ordinary waking life and are brought into fuller, more humane and sympathetic contact with others; we are awakened from dead routine to the huge potential of experience. The cinema of Truffaut, however, is not one of wish-fulfilment; problems are not solved with the ease of dreams and the claims of reality are not set aside for ever. The characters of the films may share the dream-freedom of the audience to some extent, but this freedom is always brought into conflict with the limitations of everyday reality, and the exhilaration of their experience is mingled with sadness. We as audience do not escape or avoid problems while, or after, watching the films; rather we are given totally new ways of looking at and coming to terms with them. Truffaut gives us a world very like our own world and people with our own weaknesses, desires, obsessions, failures and minor achievements, but he makes us see that world, and hence ourselves, as though for the first time, with the clarity, insight and unpredictability of a dream.

Truffaut has said that one of his main aims as a film-maker is to lead the audience to sympathise with people they would normally place in stock categories ("making [them] smaller and smaller") and then judge on the basis simply of these categories. He therefore lets us see others as we would see them if we overcame the preconceptions that govern our conscious lives. He reveals to us "anti-social" or "immoral" behaviour which suddenly becomes familiar and understandable because of its appeal to our own submerged and subconscious impulses, the needs and desires we suppress in order to get along without too much difficulty in daily life. The films are "natural," not just because they reproduce the surface of the reality around us, but because they appeal to our most truly natural instincts and longings and fears. A film like *Jules et Jim* makes life not only richer but more complicated for us, for, like a dream, it makes us aware of how pathetically tiny and inadequate the range of our conscious experience has become, and how shabby are the compromises we are constantly making with ourselves.

The central figures in most of the films are those whom we tend to place in conventional categories, either in an attempt to avoid responsibility for understanding and helping them, or through fear of recognising our own fundamental affinity with them. If we simply sum up the young Antoine Doinel as "juvenile delinquent," Julie Kohler as "murderess," Catherine as "adultress" and Jules and Jim as "parasites" or "layabouts," Charlie as "failure and/or coward" and Pierre Lachenay as "middle-aged adulterer and home-breaker," then we absolve ourselves of the need to understand them as human beings and to see how their personalities and actions reflect and interact with our own. Truffaut, however, refuses to allow us this comfort.

Julie of *La Mariée Etait en Noir* is perhaps the most difficult of these characters, both for the director to create and the audience to sympathise with. The framework of the film provides an implicit commentary on her in its contrast of a self-enclosed woman impervious to normal feelings, desires and doubts, using others coldly and deliberately for her own purposes, and the potential beauty, freedom and harmony created by music, colour and movement. But not only does Julie's narrowness carry to an extreme our own tendency to impoverish our experience of the world around us by adjusting it to suit our conscious needs, it also reflects the outlook of the men she encounters, who are equally limited, restricted and blind and, ironically, attempt to manipulate her for their own satisfaction. This affinity between killer and victim provides one basis for the subtle shifting of sympathy between them that goes on throughout the film, while the plot structure and time-scheme provide another.

The film begins abruptly with Julie's attempt at suicide, which is followed, with no indication of the time lapse that must have ensued, by the much calmer but equally intriguing scenes of her separating a pile of banknotes into five groups, placing them in a suitcase, leaving home, pretending to board a train and then slipping away immediately back into the town. The camera and the situation itself induce us to identify with Julie, though with some puzzlement as to what is going on. Then comes the enticement and sudden murder of Bliss, an episode that probably leaves us morally neutral—shocked perhaps, but still intrigued by Julie (who has already shown an apparent capacity to materialise from and disappear into nothingness) and not too upset at the demise of this handsome, debonair, but rather shallow young man.

The episode with Coral, however, is much more disturbing. We get the first explanation of Julie's actions, and her account of her husband's "murder" on their wedding day gives us an instinctive sympathy for her, but her exploitation and deception of this pathetically sad and vulnerable man, together with the sheer callousness with which she watches him die, create a repugnance that begins to distance us from her. Clément Morane is next, smug, hypocritical, complacent, ready to use Julie to satisfy his vanity and reassure himself that his political success will add even more to his sexual attractiveness. We may feel little personal sympathy for him (though the manner of his death is horrifying and he is intensely real for all his unpleasantness), but his child Cookie introduces a major complication. We probably feel more for his loss of his father than for the actual death itself, and with Cookie Julie for the first time shows possibilities of tenderness, affection, the feminine qualities that could make her an excellent wife and mother. At this stage, when our sympathies are being pulled in several directions and our attempts to puzzle out the enigma of Julie are most acute, Morane reveals that the killing was purely accidental. Julie responds with the only real grief and emotion that she displays throughout the film, as she tells him of her childhood dreams and the way in which a happiness anticipated for years was snatched away from her, but none of this alters the *fact* that the death was an accident, however careless and negligent Morane and his friends may have been, and her subsequent mechanical continuation with her plan becomes even more horrifying. The after-effects of Morane's murder tone down our reactions to some extent, however—Cookie doesn't seem too upset at losing his father and Julie's refusal to let someone else take the blame for her actions regains some sympathy for her.

The brief glimpse we have of Delvaux before his arrest doesn't make us worry too much about the fate in store for him—and in fact by this stage most of us are beginning to be at least as interested in whether and how Julie will make it to the end of her list as in the psychological complexities involved. The episode with Fergus, however, shifts the balance back towards human reactions and the fact that he is the most likeable of the men, and the one towards whom she is genuinely most inclined to relent, creates a valid emotional tension. Her solution to the problem is to close her mind again, fight down her human instincts and kill him, but her victory is so clearly anti-human that it brings triumph neither to us nor to her. Once again, however, we can escape from moral responsibility by turning our attention to the final stage of her vengeance, and for Delvaux's murder we become openly her accomplices for the first time, enjoying the ingenuity and skill with which she brings her task to a statistically and aesthetically satisfying conclusion.

The above is a grossly over-simplified account of reactions which must vary to a considerable extent from viewer to viewer, and it conveys little of the subtle coexistence of several layers of response (the idea of Julie as "an excellent wife and mother," for example, is both grotesque and touching, true and false in its context). What is inescapable, however, is the way in which the film makes it impossible for us to bring one standardised response to the whole situation, or even to any one episode or character. Julie herself is not particularly complex and little attempt is made to give her psychological depth or reality (Auden's phrase "the distortions of ingrown virginity" probably sums her up as well as anything); all that matters is that she should be a *presence* within the film which provides a catalyst for certain reactions in the other characters and in the audience (and Jeanne Moreau with her haggard beauty, her cold detachment, the glimpses she gives of warmth and tenderness beneath the self-imposed *façade,* is a most magnificent presence). The real fascination lies in the ways in which we find ourselves drawn into complicity with her, into sharing her sense of her victims as pure objects to be manipulated and disposed of *at the same time as* we are made uncomfortably aware of their reality and humanity. One side of us wishes her to succeed, with various shifting rationales and justifications as the film proceeds ("poor girl, her husband was murdered, well he wasn't murdered but Morane is a bastard anyway, in any case she let the teacher go free and wasn't it great the way she killed Delvaux and all you see is the corridor and the wedding march comes up on the soundtrack"), while another keeps reminding us that not only are these people like ourselves who are being killed but their elimination is fanatically wrong-headed. Normally a thriller, by refusing to humanise the hero's victims, gives us the

*LA MARIEE ETAIT EN NOIR: Julie as virgin bride . .*

dream-freedom to kill and punish with impunity; what Truffaut does is both to give and deny us this freedom, and this makes the film so unsettling. He does not allow us the lack of responsibility which dreams and cinema usually provide: our desire to see these people die and our very real discomfort at their death are continually coming into conflict and we cannot push the experience away into any of the categories we normally use to protect ourselves.

In all these ways the film differs markedly from the thriller by Cornell Woolrich on which it is based,[19] even though Truffaut follows the book very closely through the details of the first four murders. The changes he makes, however, alter the relationship

*... and as virgin huntress. Fergus's kitchen has blue and white patterned tiles*

between audience and characters, and audience and events so radically that a fairly straightforward and crude mystery story is turned into a work of immense complexity and fascination. Woolrich conceals the motives for Julie's actions to the very end of the book and then, in a finale full of explanations and double-twists, reveals that she has killed four innocent men and twice missed the opportunity to dispose of the right one—Bliss's and Ferguson's (the names are occasionally different in book and film) friend Corey, who had murdered her husband in revenge for a business double-cross. In addition she fails to kill her final victim and is arrested by a detective who has been working on her case from the beginning of the story and to whose activities a great deal of attention is paid throughout. The book then concentrates on a fairly mechanical suspense structure ("Who is this woman?" "Why is she killing all these men?"), with several deliberate and at times very crude false trails and suspects, concentrating to a large extent on the problems of the police in hunting her down, and closing with twists of fact and identity that "surprise" (or infuriate) the reader. There is none of the involvement and complicity of the audience created by Truffaut's early revelation of her motive and his making the men responsible for the killing even though by accident, and nothing of the disconcerting insight into our own moral nature which the film gives us. The book goes through a series of mechanical reversals (held mostly to the end) that affect the characters primarily and have a purely momentary and superficial impact on the reader; the film progresses through a series of shifts which constantly interact with and draw in the audience.

In the novel, milieu and characters are uniformly unsympathetic. The settings are bleak and sordid, the language and motives of all the characters crude and coarse, and there is no attempt to humanise or give complexity to any of the victims. All are one-dimensional figures put up simply to be knocked down as ingeniously as possible and it is impossible to spare a second thought for any of them—even Cookie emerges as such an unlikeable brat that it never occurs to the reader to worry, or even wonder, about the effect of his father's. death on him. Their reactions towards Julie are crudely physical (even the supposedly idealistic Mitchell—the Coral of the book—has a string of third-rate sexual conquests behind him and a whining girl friend competing with Julie for his attention) and she responds with blatant sexual provocations. There is no hint of a more subtle relationship even with the artist Ferguson or of any weakening on her part towards him. Ironically the only character in the film who corresponds to the figures created by Woolrich is Delvaux, who is Truffaut's own creation entirely (the Holmes of the book is a writer of romantic novels whose place is in any case taken by the disguised detective). Truffaut's transformation of the whole of the last episode and ending of the book allows him to present Delvaux as a dummy whose killing we can look forward to in gleeful anticipation—with the concomitant complexities already described—while giving the other victims their full and disturbing measure of humanity. And there is no equivalent in the novel to the harmonious rhythmic framework Truffaut sets up or to the subtle use of clothes and colours—Julie's clothes are seldom described in any detail and though she sometimes wears white and sometimes black, she wears blue on her visit to Moran [sic]. She also eats and drinks heartily and only vanishes to keep out of the way of the police.

While remaining faithful to the outline and events of the first four-fifths of the book, Truffaut changes its emphasis in a way which is both unsettling and illuminating. The sordid and mechanical "naturalism" of the book fails to bring any of the characters or events to life in any very challenging way; while Truffaut's romanticism and the mysterious and dreamlike atmosphere which he creates combine with his typical attention to the details of human experience to produce a work of complex and evocative beauty, for whose subtleties the original can take little credit.

Even though she is so much more interesting than her counterpart in the novel (with whom we can never identify, for we know nothing about her or her motives), Truffaut's Julie makes few demands on our sympathy—the point of the film is our simultaneous complicity with and revulsion from her, making us uncomfortably aware of potentials within us which we prefer not to acknowledge. Jeanne Moreau plays her role, or roles admirably, incarnating for each man his own limited version of the feminine ideal. Yet her ability to provide so many facets of the ideal gives her an almost supernatural or at least superhuman quality that links her to the figure of Catherine in *Jules et Jim* (also, and superbly, portrayed by Jeanne Moreau). Catherine provides a version of the ideal for Jules, Jim, Albert and innumerable other men, and is variously described as a "queen" or a "goddess" on several occasions. Again Truffaut makes no attempt to explain her or to account for the fascination she exerts; he simply presents her, persuades us to accept and thus believe in her, and lets us see the consequences of these people (and ourselves) being what they are. The film communicates the experience of the characters so vividly that we cannot help accepting them, and at the same time takes us into a dream world where they act with a freedom, a lack of responsibility, commitment and consequence, which must appeal to the deepest impulses in all of us. Their behaviour is anti-social (or at least extra-social—we perhaps tend to confuse the two) and self-indulgent, but no one seems to be hurt by it and we are lulled and charmed into acceptance and some kind of identification. But just when we have submitted fully and begun, like the characters, to treat the dream world and the real world as one, reality catches up and the dream begins to crumble away, jealousy, pain, frustration and cruelty reassert themselves. We are brought back into the kind of situations we all have to contend with, but with the potential and anguish of the lost dream world making it impossible to accept the "real" world as adequate or satisfactory.

All the characters are responsible for the failure of the dream and yet all are innocent, for each has his reasons. We are not given the satisfaction of a scapegoat, instead we see people who, with our consent and approbation, have tried to live free of conventions and restrictions and are now forced to come to terms with elements within themselves which they thought they had gone beyond—and we see this, not with the complacent satisfaction that conventional wisdom has shown itself to be "right" in the end, but with sadness that the experiment has failed and that limitations exist after all, however much we may wish to deny this. But the limitations can now be seen in a new perspective and from this perspective, rather than from the old one, it may be possible to do something about them— or at least to try.

Catherine is the easiest target for scapegoat, for she most easily fits the conventional stereotypes of immorality, especially when seen in the pre-First World War context of the film. Certainly she is egotistical and selfish, she refuses to accept the consequences of her actions and, in declaring her freedom from conventional restraints, simply reverses moral categories and judgements to suit herself—applying one set of rules (or rather no rules) to herself and another to other people, and demanding a freedom for herself that she refuses her lovers. All these contribute to the failure of the relationship and indicate that freedom is not simply a matter of changing the rules to suit oneself. Jules is the weakest of the three and the most vulnerable; he has an inner need for security and fidelity, but attempts to deny this in order to play the game as the others wish it. The result of trying to conform to non-conformity is that Catherine comes to despise him for his in-between stance and shows her contempt, leading him to retreat into alternating cynicism and self-pity (as his aim of writing a love story in which the characters would be insects indicates). Jim is both stronger and more ruthless and his use of Gilberte as a refuge and weapon against Catherine parallels her use of Albert to spite or humiliate the other two—a reminder again that absolute "freedom" in accordance with one's own standards means that all have to conform with these standards to avoid exploitation and betrayal. Despite their genuine affection and concern for one another, and especially the friendship between the two men that Truffaut conveys so economically and so well, the inability of all three to understand themselves and their desires, and their refusal to adjust to circumstances or to the needs of others, forces them inexorably into a pattern of hurting, humiliating and finally destroying one another. Yet we cannot ultimately blame or condemn any of them: Catherine is to be admired for her intensity, passion, vitality, her desire to live life as fully and completely as possible; Jules is placed in an intolerable situation, yet manages to act with devotion, tenderness and forgiveness; Jim retains integrity, honesty and forthrightness throughout. What gives all of them dignity and fascination is their attempt to be true at all costs to their inner selves, to the desires and needs and impulses which we all share but are normally too cowardly, lazy, conventional or cynical to do more than fulfil in dreams.

The kind of compromise made by most people is represented by Pierre Lachenay in *La Peau Douce*. He is inwardly, though not at first consciously, dissatisfied with the kind of life he is leading, but instead of trying to cut free from it and to reject or transcend its limitations, he attempts to get round them. He wants both security and freedom, outward adherence to conventional standards and secret avoidance of them, wife and mistress simultaneously, just as later he wants mistress and daughter. Little of this, however, is conscious choice; it is more the result of inertia and the refusal to make decisions. He prefers to drift along with situations as they arise, hoping that things will work themselves out and allowing others to take the initiative (a trait that is physically very well caught as Franca attempts to make him *decide* something near the end and seizes and shakes him as though he were some kind of limp rag dummy). In all these aspects, and in his desire for freedom without the responsibilities that must accompany it, he is very "normal" and very human, and any attempt to pass judgement on him must make us uneasily aware that we are also condemning ourselves.

Pierre wants the benefits of conformity and non-conformity simultaneously, without taking risks, and he muddles his way to disaster showing little of the flair or energy of Catherine and Jim, who at least make a clear and honest choice of the kind of life they want. Unlike them, he is gentle and hesitant, wanting to please everyone all the time and reluctant to hurt anyone, but the inevitable consequence of this is that he never commits himself whole-heartedly, never tells the full truth until it is too late and succeeds only in wounding by default. He is tied down by daily affairs and responsibilities and these are to a large extent at the root of the failure of the affair with Nicole, but he is equally inhibited by his desire to play along both with social conventions and with inner needs that inevitably run counter to these.

The basic situation of the film is one that cinema and television usually treat as pure wish-fulfilment, perhaps adding an unhappy ending as a sop to the moral hypocrisy of the audience, but investing it with a good deal of spurious glamour along the way and imposing on it intensely "meaningful" relationships and experiences. Once again Truffaut refuses to play along with this: the dream potential is there, but it is never fulfilled; our conventional expectations are aroused but not given conventional satisfactions. The treatment is uncompromisingly down-to-earth, emphasising the mundane matters of place, time and opportunity that the standard versions of the story blandly ignore. Nothing goes right for very long, and even the usual roles played by the women are reversed: it is the wife who is passionate and sexually aggressive and the mistress who is cold and detached, just as between Pierre and Nicole it is the man who wants security and marriage while the woman has taken over the traditional masculine freedom. Pierre feels vaguely committed to and guilty about Franca, but even on the brink of disaster he cannot make a clear-cut decision about how to treat her (told by a friend that he should try to make it up with her he mutters, "Yes, I'll do it next week," then, prodded into action, he waits outside an occupied 'phone booth, surveying the attractive girl inside in a way suggesting that he would drift in her direction if she gave him the slightest encouragement). This kind of behaviour inevitably frustrates all Franca's attempts to get through to him; she is driven to killing him, however, by the double tensions of becoming absolutely certain of his infidelity and then being pestered in the street by a man very like Pierre who tries to pick her up. When she rounds viciously on this man, recognising in him her husband's self-deprecating smile, his complacency and his dishonesty, she pours out on him all the pent-up frustration and misery which Pierre has never been around long enough to listen to. Nicole is both less vital and less attractive, but she cannot be blamed for what happens any more than Pierre or Franca can. She is every middle-aged man's dream-girl, beautiful, accessible and free-living, but she is at the same time perfectly honest about herself and it is Pierre's refusal to see her as a real person and

Truffaut's *LA SIRENE DU MISSISSIPI*. Catherine Deneuve and Jean-Paul Belmondo. Photo: United Artists.

*Truffaut's LA MARIEE ETAIT EN NOIR. Charles Denner at the easel. Jeanne Moreau, dressed as Diana, in the background. Photo: United Artists.*

his persistence in trying to live a dream with her which prevent him from reading the signals that are plain to see from the beginning. Conventionally Pierre is the most "guilty," but such questions become irrelevant as, through Jean Desailly's beautifully controlled performance, he reveals himself as too human, too confused, too vulnerable, too like ourselves for us to pass judgement. Where Jules, Catherine and Jim try to make the real world conform to their dream version of it and inevitably and bravely fail, Pierre makes the more usual attempt to bring the dream into harmony with the limited and narrow world of his daily experience; his failure is less glorious but strikes uncomfortably close to home.

Charlie Koller of *Tirez sur le Pianiste* attempts like the trio of *Jules et Jim* to live apart from society, but instead of moving into a wider, freer, more vital world, he retreats into one that is even more enclosed and restricted than that of normal experience. He makes more of a conscious choice than Pierre does, but is equally unable to commit himself firmly to one course of action. Having failed his wife in a moment of extreme crisis, he wishes to avoid hurting himself or others in future, but chooses a method which ensures that he will go on repeating his earlier mistake rather than correcting it. He tries to withdraw from social and personal relationships as far as possible and maintains a *façade* of aloofness and impassivity. Yet at the same time he continues to make himself available to others by living and working in their world, assuming that they will recognise and accept the dissociation he himself makes between his private, mental world and that in which he earns his bread. (It is also perhaps a subconscious acceptance of his real need of others.) But this doesn't work; others are fascinated, puzzled or antagonised by him and attempt to draw him out, either for their own advantage, as Chico and his brothers do, or with the aim of helping him, as Lena does. Family loyalty, gratitude, love, guilt, all of them emotions he had thought he had suppressed, combine to make him respond to their promptings, but his refusal to acknowledge the effect of these emotions on him till too late ensures that he never makes the right decision at the right time. He allows others to take the initiative for him and tries to opt out of responsibility until circumstances drag him in at a stage when he has no control over the course of events and can do nothing to prevent disaster. At the end of the film the introduction of a new barmaid and the sight of the impassive Charlie playing the same tune he has played throughout indicate that nothing has really changed for him and he will slip inexorably back into the old pattern. He shares with Jules, Jim and Catherine the assumption that his telling himself that he no longer has certain emotions will automatically dispel them, and with Pierre the belief that if he sits tight and does nothing, things will somehow work themselves out. The result is an impasse in which commitment leads inexorably to disaster and lack of commitment proves impossible.

Despite Charlie's obvious weaknesses and self-deception, and the sordid surroundings, people and conversation in which he chooses to move, it is impossible for us either to judge him or to dissociate ourselves from him. The style of the film disorients in a way which makes us ready to look at things with a fresh eye, and mingled with the shabbiness and weariness of the characters are humour and insight; people come vividly alive with very human weaknesses, needs, disappointments, self-protective deceptions and *façades* that in the long run don't fool anyone, least of all themselves. Charlie's mask of world-heavy impassivity is constantly being knocked aside by the interior monologue which reveals his fundamental insecurity and vulnerability. His solution to the risks of life and involvement with other people is to make himself "smaller and smaller," to retreat into a "little circle" which shuts off the outside world as far as

162

possible. As the other characters show, this is a not uncommon device, yet it is his failure to succeed with it, his acceptance of his need and responsibility for others which, paradoxically, humanises him, and an ability to take Charlie into the worlds we ourselves have created and to accept our affinity with him can humanise us.

Truffaut, incidentally, follows the events and characterisation of David Goodis's taut and atmospheric thriller *Down There*[16] remarkably closely throughout, changing very little in terms of action and personality. The changes he does make, however, are in the direction of humanising Charlie, making him more vulnerable and innocent, and also more comic, than he is in the novel (a process which takes in most of the other characters

*Antoine behind bars in LES 400 COUPS*

as well), and the shifts of tone and the bizarre juxtapositions which give the film its unique flavour have no counterpart in the book.

The three films about Antoine Doinel make less demands for readjustment of conventional attitudes on the part of the audience. Antoine, perfectly incarnated by Jean-Pierre Léaud in the various stages of his career, is the ideal Truffaut hero—impulsive, naïve, shy, insecure, generous—qualities which have difficulty in adjusting to the impersonality and fundamental dishonesty of contemporary life. The conflict is most acute in *Les 400 Coups,* where Antoine is constantly brought up against social restrictions in the shape of school, family, police and reformatory (restrictions which we have either helped to establish or, by accepting, have helped to maintain); he attempts to escape or compromise with these with little success and is finally put out of the way because society can think of nothing better to do with him.

Antoine lies, steals, stays away from school and, as a result, society applies the category of "juvenile delinquent" to him and assumes that its responsibility for him ends with this categorisation. We are part of that society, but in our other role of viewers of the film we find it impossible to sum up and dispose of Antoine in this way. He has become too uncomfortably human and in a way that completely avoids sentimentality or special pleading. He is not particularly bad or rebellious, or brilliant or sensitive; he is simply a normal boy whose very real intelligence and alertness, his capacity for emotional warmth and openness, are systematically stifled in order to make him conform to social requirements as quickly and smoothly as possible. It is a process which all children undergo and from which few of them escape unscathed, for contemporary society has no need, time or desire to attempt to develop the individual potential of each child. Antoine is just a little bit more unlucky and a little bit more resistent than most, and the honesty and directness with which his decline is charted convince far more effectively than dramatically contrived situations and outright denunciation could have. He slips imperceptibly from behaviour which society will ostensibly disapprove of but nevertheless tolerate, to actions, no worse in themselves, which it suddenly and inexplicably decides to punish (his father does nothing about his stealing from his schoolmates, yet brings the full force of the law down on him for stealing a typewriter). Neither his family nor any outside authority ever attempts to make clear just what is expected of him, and he is placed in an ambiguous status between child and adult throughout: his mother baths him as though he were a small child and sends him out of the room during a family quarrel, but he is allowed to sit at table while his father talks of sexual permutations in office politics and then goes on to speak admiringly of the kind of economic dishonesty and double-dealing to which society is prepared to turn a blind eye. In jail he is housed with an adult male criminal until three prostitutes arrive and he is placed in a cell of his own. He is sent to reformatory rather than to prison, but at the reformatory the psychiatrist takes it for granted that he has had sexual experience (presumably with the kind of prostitutes whose very presence was so injurious to his morals earlier). His ambiguous standing in the outside world is most vividly conveyed in the scene of the puppet show, to which Antoine and René take a tiny girl they have picked up, but where they sit at the back and discuss how to steal typewriters while little children all around them scream and gasp with delight at Punch and Judy.

The atmosphere and behaviour of the adult world give Antoine few trustworthy clues about what is expected of him, and there is little to give him confidence in adult justice, consistency, honesty or reliability. It is a world full of pettiness and quarrels,

*LES 400 COUPS: the school room and teacher*

boring and purposeless routines, and a stifling deadness and half-subdued hostility seem to hang over almost all personal relationships (despite his father's later assurance that he had never struck Antoine, the boy automatically puts up an arm to defend himself from a blow as the teacher approaches him to see what is written on the wall behind the blackboard). Yet there is little deliberate malice at work and the authorities are not turned into tyrants or bullies; they are either simply doing their best within the narrow framework provided for them by regulations or their own mental horizon, or are too harassed and preoccupied to have much time for him. His parents are in almost as much of a trap as he is, obsessed by the need to obtain money to keep or raise their standing in the economic and social system; his teachers are disillusioned and overworked, having given up long ago the unequal fight against overcrowding, boredom and squalor; the police face much the same problems and answer them by relying entirely on a routine and standardised response to every situation; the judge tries to be sympathetic but has no time to provide for the whims and needs of each individual. Set against what we have seen of Antoine's vitality and resourcefulness, his capacity for deep and spontaneous emotion, the very *ordinariness* of all this takes on unexpected force: we are brought face to face with what is happening every day and all around us. It is not possible for us to judge or condemn Antoine, and even sympathy is no longer an adequate response; neither can we shuffle off responsibility on to an anonymous and nonexistent "They." The drearily mechanical and unjust adult world of the film, with its casual and callous destruction of human potential, is that which we ourselves have created and it is one we choose to live in as long as we lack the imagination to dream a better one.*

The older Antoine of *L'Amour à Vingt Ans* and *Baisers Volés* moves in a less bitter and hostile world, but still has little ability to adapt himself to what is expected of him. By conventional standards he is a failure—in *L'Amour à Vingt Ans* he fails to get anywhere with the girl, either physically or emotionally; in *Baisers Volés* he loses one job after another and seems totally lacking in the maturity, stability and sense of responsibility which are normally taken as signs of successful social adaptation, and, though he wins the girl this time, it is the result solely of her taking the initiative. The effect of this, however, is not to make us despise Antoine; he emerges as such a human

*Truffaut's original intention was to make the film rather more comic and light-hearted than it in fact turned out. A recent re-issue of the film replaced ten minutes or so, mainly of school scenes, which apparently shift the balance more in this direction.

and likeable figure that the result is to show how totally irrelevant socially-determined criteria are in evaluating the worth of any individual.

Both films are quiet and relaxed in style and are presented with exceptional honesty as to the truth of emotional experience. Truffaut deals with very ordinary situations and characters, but refuses to subscribe to the subtle wish-fulfilment, the re-writing and re-working within our memories which takes over when most of us, even (and perhaps especially) writers and film-makers, attempt to re-create our youthful indiscretions. He shows the reality which we prefer to smooth over and to re-interpret in a manner more satisfactory and creditable to our present selves—but he does this with humour rather than bitterness. It is a fairly common assumption today that "realism" in art should be equated with "savage exposure"; Truffaut's "realism" is of the kind that unobtrusively puts to rights our unbalanced and distorted perspective on human experience and places neglected human values back firmly where they belong, at the centre. Antoine then is as fumbling, inept and opportunistic in sexual relationships as most people are at his stage, and Truffaut shows the misunderstandings, antagonisms and selfishness that are to be found in even the most successful love affair. He avoids not only an obviously false slickness and over-sophistication but the more insidious temptation to make human and sexual relationships in art easier, more satisfactory and gratifying to the *ego* than they ever are in real life. Unlike the major characters in some of the other films, Antoine and Christine are easy to like and sympathise with immediately and there is no need for any radical readjustment of sympathy towards them; the film makes its real impact through working within and yet, by its basic honesty, undermining the "young love" convention. The final effect of the film can be very disconcerting if we allow it to penetrate our own personal haze of sentimental and self-gratifying reminiscence and if we can resist the temptation of condescending to Antoine by reminding ourselves how much more accomplished and successful we, of course, were (or are) at his age.

In most of Truffaut's films the effect of the style and the presentation of characters is to create in us an openness and responsiveness to the variety of life and experience available beyond the limits we choose for ourselves or allow to be set for us. We are brought to recognise our own affinity with characters we would normally see as having little relationship with ourselves, or made to see the inadequacies of conventional modes of existence when these are placed in conjunction with characters who try to go beyond them. At the same time Truffaut doesn't provide us with easy answers by simply reversing the conventional injunctions ("conform!", "work!", "earn money!", "get married!") and assuming that if we do none of these things then somehow everything will be very much better. There is a constant tension between the inhibiting, restrictive moral, social and economic world that is everyday life, and the dream world of freedom where responsibilities and confinements can be ignored. The impulse of the films is towards the dream, and one result of them is to make us aware of the limitations and to respond towards them in a new way.

The exception, once again, is *Fahrenheit 451*. Truffaut's choice of this subject is not completely inexplicable for his love of books is evident in almost every film. In *Les 400 Coups* and *Baisers Volés* Antoine is an avid reader of Balzac, and the leading male characters in *Jules et Jim* and *La Peau Douce* are writers who are constantly reading, referring to or commenting on literary works. *Jules et Jim* also has a newsreel clip of Hitler's burning of the books and the characters express horror and disgust at this portent. The mental atmosphere of *Fahrenheit 451*, as Truffaut makes quite clear by his setting, is not that of

*The non-verbal world of FAHRENHEIT 451—Linda and Montag*

the future so much as that of today, in the sense that the central features and assumptions which make book-burning possible are present, though submerged, in the contemporary world. Recent developments in North American society that have made it fashionable and profitable for teachers of literature to express open scorn and contempt for books give his conclusion considerable authority. (I am referring less to Marshall McLuhan, much of whose work I have found stimulating and important, than to some of the more nimble adherents to his bandwagon.) However, the assumptions behind Bradbury's novel are, in their own way, equally facile and simple-minded, and the structure of the novel makes Truffaut's normal avoidance of easy value-judgements quite impossible. The characters divide inexorably into "right" and "wrong," and Truffaut's uneasy attempt to give them slightly more reality and avoid clear-cut moralising by making Montag rather stupid and the book-people ultimately futile (his *Journal* suggests that this is deliberate), though laudable, merely confuses the issues and works against basic premises which the rest of the film accepts. The characters never take on enough reality or self-sufficiency to surprise or interest to any extent, and Truffaut's well-publicised disagreements with Oskar Werner resulted in the latter giving a performance that falls well short of the subtlety and depth of his earlier portrayal of Jules, while Julie Christie goes through her standard routine of alternating radiance with sullenness and contributing little else. The film is one that sets out its premises at the beginning and then, despite some hesitations, proceeds simply to re-inforce them, in a way both alien to Truffaut's cast of mind and tediously over-explicit in itself.

Perhaps the most characteristic single feature of the people Truffaut creates on the screen is *loneliness*. Only Julie Kohler and Charlie Koller choose their isolation, and both do so as a result of seeing their dreams of happiness and companionship shattered; most of the others have it forced on them by their own weaknesses or by the conditions of contemporary life. But the films are by no means as sombre as this might imply, and Truffaut is far from presenting us with the standard *clichés* about alienation or lack of communication. His people *are* lonely, they *do* find it difficult to find the right kind of relationship with others, and yet Truffaut can communicate better than any other film director the quality of friendship and love, the moments of joy and fulfilment that all the characters experience, even though they may lack or eventually be deprived of the possibilities of permanent association with others. It is the balance between the communication of the very real achievements of friendship (as in *Jules et Jim*) and love (especially in *Baisers Volés*) and

171

the honest realisation that, despite these, people remain essentially alone, locked in their own worlds, that gives his films their beauty and their poignancy.

For Antoine in *Les 400 Coups* family life is a farce, school an impersonal and irrelevant bore, and the outside world as a whole hostile and untrustworthy. The only person he can turn to is René, but he, being also a child, cannot help him in a crisis, and one of the most moving scenes in the film shows René, having cycled out to the reformatory, being denied access to Antoine while his mother is allowed to enter and tell him smugly that she and his father disown him. At the end of the film Antoine is left completely and utterly alone, with no one and no place to turn to. René reappears in *L'Amour à Vingt*

*LES 400 COUPS: René (Patrick Auffay) tries in vain to visit Antoine in the reformatory . . .*

*Ans,* but Antoine is now more concerned with winning Colette, who is fundamentally indifferent to him, and in *Baisers Volés* he seems to have no close friends at all and those who do appear out of the past have drifted irrevocably away from him. Certainly there is the compensation of Christine, though the ending of the film manages to place the ultimate permanence of the relationship in some doubt, and in Christine's parents Truffaut shows marriage and family life in a better light than usual.

Antoine's drift from friendship with other men to girls to marriage is reflected in *Jules et Jim* as the two men move steadily further apart in the course of the film, though their continuing affection for each other allows each to deprive himself of Catherine for the other's sake. By the end the closeness between

*. . . while his mother comes to tell him that his family disown him*

them is virtually dissipated; unable at the beginning of the film to live without each other's company, they can now spend several years without seeing or writing to each other. In the sexual relationship it is Jules's hurt and loneliness that is dwelt on most, yet it is Jim who is seen most often alone towards the conclusion. Catherine herself is finally brought to realise that her independence, her desire to be free of ties and responsibilities also entails that no one feels any particular obligation or concern about her and that she has no moral claims on Jim after all (though she can take him with her into death).

In the first four features, one central character survives alone at the end (in order, Antoine, Charlie, Jules, Franca), with little or nothing to look forward to. The death of the other two has freed Jules from the vicious circle they had been caught in, but he cannot disown or escape from what has been the central experience of his whole life. Charlie has gone through a cycle of alienation—partial commitment—hesitation—full commitment—loss which repeats his earlier one and seems destined to stay with him for ever. Franca in avenging herself on Pierre has wiped out all that gave her life meaning, and Pierre himself had gained little from an illicit affair full of continual frustration. In *Les Mistons* Gérard's death leaves Bernadette alone at the end, giving the children who had persecuted the lovers while Gérard was alive their first vague insight into the meaning of suffering and loss. Montag in *Fahrenheit 451* can make no contact with his wife, who lives in a world dominated by the phoney intimacy of the global village; he is disliked and distrusted by his colleagues and superiors, and even the relationship with Clarisse has almost no personal warmth and seems to offer little for the future. Julie Kohler's love for her dead David has turned to something morbid and obsessive in the light of her behaviour in the film and her capacities for warmth and tenderness are coldly distorted to enable her to attract and destroy her victims.

The minor characters move in the same kind of world and share the same experiences, and one of the most impressive features of Truffaut's films is his ability to make every individual come vividly to life, however trivial his role in the plot may be, through attention to detail, gestures, actions, speech patterns— above all through a basic respect and love for human beings. The barman in *Tirez sur le Pianiste* is both repulsive and pathetic, keenly aware of his own deficiencies ("Women don't like me because of my ugly mug," he explains to Charlie) and of the ultimate futility of his existence. His mistress's bitter "Do you call this living?" in reply to a remark by Lena catches the routine dead-end despair of relationships that have long since lost all meaning but are held together by habit or fear of solitude—relationships like those of René's parents in *Les 400 Coups* and the two detectives in *Baisers Volés*. Antoine's parents live in much the same way, spiritually dead to each other and with only flashes of sexual desire to bring them alive again (vividly and sensually created as the family returns happily from their outing to the cinema* and the father fondles his wife's breasts as she hangs up her coat). The most frightening and explicit scene of sexual deadness is in *Jules et Jim* where Jim on a visit to Paris meets an old acquaintance who shows

---

*To see, according to the mother, *Paris Nous Appartient*, Jacques Rivette's film, which Truffaut co-produced, but which wasn't completed till 1960, a year after *Les 400 Coups* appeared. In any case the three of them come out falling over themselves with laughter, which is not exactly the reaction most people have to Rivette's brilliant film, and the title on the marquee outside clearly indicates that they have seen something else. Truffaut has his share of *Nouvelle Vague* in-jokes; another is the *Cahiers du Cinéma* poster on the back of a van which the gangsters' car follows briefly in *Tirez sur le Pianiste*.

him his current mistress: "It's no use talking to her, she won't answer. . . . She's not a half-wit, she's just empty. There's nothing in there. She's just a thing. . . . a beautiful object. She's sex personified, pure sex."[2] And he raps dispassionately on the girl's forehead to prove his point. (This scene, incidentally, has no counterpart in the novel).

The sense of loneliness is strongest in *La Mariée Etait en Noir* and *Baisers Volés*, each of which has a vivid gallery of solitaries, people who may be arrogant, pathetic or hypocritical, but who are given full humanity by their vulnerability, their closeness to pain and deprivation. My own favourites are Robert Coral with his furtive, futile vanity (peering into a second mirror held behind his head to make sure that he is combing his hair over his bald spot), his nervous and naïvely complacent delight at the attention which Julie delusively shows him; and the two roles played by Michel Lonsdale. As Clément Morane in *La Mariée Etait en Noir* he is delightfully repulsive, one of those figures with almost no redeeming qualities who is nevertheless so fully and lovingly brought to life that one can only revel in the representation. In M. Tabard of *Baisers Volés* we have someone with a *façade* of detached assurance and complete emotional control, under which lurks the frightening and justified suspicion that no one likes him. He is both sad and comic, and Truffaut gives an added and honest dimension to his character by showing him as someone whom it is genuinely very hard to like (he leaps touchily to Hitler's defence by reminding his mocking wife that he was a landscape painter, not a house painter) but whom it is also impossible to condemn. There are, however, many others such as the magician's friend, whose hurt and bewildered refusal to believe in his desertion leads to a scene in which knockabout farce and emotional loss and pain are characteristically interwined. Even the gangsters of *Tirez sur le Pianiste* with their jerky, automaton-like movements, their

*TIREZ SUR LE PIANISTE: Fido (Richard Kanayan) is kidnapped by the gangsters*

vague sense of better days and lost opportunities, their ineffectual imitation of actions and gestures from faintly-recollected B-movies, and their attempts to impress others with the need to take them seriously, have a humanity which somehow co-exists with the fact that they end by killing Lena. (In all these respects they differ markedly from the tough, efficient killers of the book.)

Although loneliness and loss are central factors in the world Truffaut creates, the films themselves are never depressing. He is well aware that most people live in worlds of their own, choosing to hold on to what is familiar and safe, however unsatisfactory, rather than taking the risk of losing this in an attempt to find something better. Some are forced into this through their own weakness or personal deficiencies that they are unable to overcome; others could perhaps break out but are too cowardly or inert to make the attempt. Truffaut himself refuses to make generalisations or categories in order to define people; he insists on humanising each individual to show both his affinities with others (and with ourselves) and the uniqueness which makes every person matter to himself and which makes the waste and hurt involved in each particular life even more telling. There is no condescension or sentimentality and he has a wonderful gift for infusing warmth into the portrayal even of unsympathetic people and for showing failure without being depressing or patronising.

Yet not everyone is a failure and many of the characters attempt to escape from the traps set up all around them. Society is seen as basically repressive, offering little satisfaction in terms of work or social achievement, for these quickly become dead routines and even writers succumb to habit and inertia (neither Jules nor Jim seems satisfied with his writing and though Jim is more successful, the actual merit of his work is left unstated. Pierre is a literary lion whose reputation is built solely on his commentary on the work of other writers). Fulfilment has to be sought outside society, in personal relationships; although these offer real joy and satisfaction they inevitably come into conflict with social requirements and are either destroyed or muted. Yet while the joy lasts Truffaut conveys it with a zest and gaiety which no other film-maker has surpassed—especially in the first half of *Jules et Jim* and countless moments of *Les Mistons, Les 400 Coups, Tirez sur le Pianiste* and *Baisers Volés.* Even in the ostensibly more bleak situations of *La Peau Douce, Fahrenheit 451* and *La Mariée Etait en Noir* the films are constantly infused with humour, lightness, affection, vitality, rhythmic grace, visual beauty and a musical commen-

178

tary which together allow for sadness but not solemnity or tediousness.

Genuine friendship is rare and difficult and tends to be destroyed or interfered with by social pressures or sexual distractions. But where it exists and while it lasts Truffaut handles it with unaffected ease and naturalness. The quality of the relationships between Jules and Jim, and Antoine and René, is conveyed by their actions, the way they *do* things together, things often ridiculous or childish but spontaneous and unforced. Friendship is rarely verbalised in the films and false or strained friendships, such as that between Pierre and Michel in *La Peau Douce* or Antoine's meeting with old acquaintances in *Baisers Volés*, are presented purely as a matter of words. Another kind

*Friendship: René and Antoine in LES 400 COUPS*

of friendship springs up between Antoine and the parents of his girl friends. In *L'Amour à Vingt Ans* this is both touching and—taking into account the girl's indifferences to him—ridiculous; in *Baisers Volés* it co-exists with, rather than replaces, his relationship with Christine, but in both cases it is expressed in the unaffected warmth and openness with which they accept him and make him feel at home, almost always giving him something to eat and drink as soon as he arrives. (This behaviour takes on particular effectiveness in the light of what we know of Antoine's own home life.)

Sexual relationships are more pervasive and more complex. Truffaut's men tend to be shy and passive, allowing the women to take the initiative and to dominate. The women have vitality, energy, a desire for new experiences which the men usually lack, harassed as they are by a sense of inadequacy and the routines and pressures of daily existence, and possessing often a fundamental gentleness denied the more ruthless females. Whereas the men find it difficult to disengage themselves sufficiently from the complexities of social existence and from the roles which they are constantly assuming to cope with these, the women have fewer ties and inhibitions and seem able to devote themselves more wholeheartedly to the pursuit of sensual or emotional satisfaction. It is not simply a question of relative social freedom, however, for Lena and Nicole both have full-time jobs and both have more vitality than their male partners—though Truffaut does seem to be commenting on the way in which the contemporary male has allowed his traditional freedom of sexual initiative (based on his economic and social strength as bread-winner) to be submerged in the futilities and trivialities of the routine of work, at the same time as the female has used her growing economic independence and achievement of social status to claim a freedom of her own. It is equally a matter of moral inhibitions and the films seem to reflect a con-

*Woman dominant: Jim (left) and Jules carry Catherine down to the beach in JULES ET JIM*

temporary loss of confidence and confusion in the male as to exactly what his masculine role now amounts to, as women steadily encroach on more and more of what used to be male territory. The traits Truffaut presents are also, however, aspects of personality which can exist independently of wider social patterns, and which he obviously finds congenial, as his constant return to and variation of them shows.

Catherine is the most ruthless and most domineering of all Truffaut's women (if we except Julie, whose function is simply to kill men). She controls her relationship with the two men from the very beginning, is very conscious of doing so and exerts her authority as a matter of principle. It is she who makes the choices and decisions and rules quite openly as their

*Some of Truffaut's lovers: Jim and Catherine in JULES ET JIM (above), Pierre and Nicole in LA PEAU DOUCE (below) . . .*

*. . . Linda and Montag in FAHRENHEIT 451 (above), and Christine and Antoine in BAISERS VOLES*

queen, taking on and discarding other men as it suits her when she wants to punish them or keep them in their place. But all this makes the relationship totally one-sided and unbalanced, and the effect is finally to wear herself and the others out under the constant pressure which she exerts. She refuses ever to allow things to take their own course or to proceed at their own pace; there is a sense that the men are continually being tested and placed on trial and the result is nervous exhaustion and then a growing resentment. She is imperious and arbitrary on principle, acting on unexplained whims or according to her strictly personal sense of justice ("Pay off your debts and start again from scratch," or "We mustn't both suffer at the same time. When you stop, I shall start again.") She tries to control life, to make it take the pattern which suits her, but despite her own affinity to a "force of nature," as Jules puts it, life and people are too complex to be manipulated in this way. Yet her vitality and fascination are such that she almost succeeds in pulling it off, and it is easy to understand what it is that keeps both Jules and Jim tied to her, despite frustration and humiliation: Jim in particular is stronger than most of Truffaut's other men, yet Catherine offers challenges, mysteries and rewards impossible for him to evade or for Jules to escape.

Julie Kohler carries Catherine's traits to an extreme, consciously and deliberately manipulating human reactions to suit herself, but in a far more cold-blooded way and for a different purpose. Her aim is much more limited than Catherine's and she is much more successful: the men succumb meekly to her, ironically imagining that they are using her to gratify their own wishes, while she simply exploits their weakness and vanity. Only Fergus, with his genuine and spontaneous declaration of love for her, makes her hesitate, though not for long. Certainly her actions are a constant and deliberate distortion of a nature that shows itself capable of normal human responses and desires, but her role pushes to its farthest point what seems to be Truffaut's habitual view of the female dominance in sexual relationships.

Though it is Pierre in *La Peau Douce* who makes the first move in his affair with Nicole, it is she who makes all the real decisions, 'phoning him back in the hotel when he was prepared to give up and forget the whole business and ensuring that the affair will continue by slipping him her 'phone number at a stage when he was ready to walk away out of her life without committing himself. Yet, having attracted him, she remains fairly distant throughout and finally leaves him, telling him that he was foolish to expect anything permanent from her (she says this with compassion but without any real understanding or concern for what she has done to his life). At the same time that he is failing to put his adulterous relationship on a satisfactory basis, Pierre is constantly under pressure from his wife with her demand for the involvement and response which he is himself failing to win from Nicole.

Lena in *Tirez sur le Pianiste* takes the initiative with Charlie, waiting for him outside the bar, inviting him to walk her home, avoiding his first tentative advances, but later, when she is sure of him, quietly leading him back to her room and bed. She makes a conscious and determined attempt to mould and "restore" him, to take over (with the best of intentions) the direction and shaping of his life. (In both films the authoritative role of the woman is underlined in tongue-in-cheek manner by her instructions to the man to get her some stockings on his way home.)

Antoine is manipulated and controlled by all the women to whom he makes advances. Colette in *L'Amour à Vingt Ans* plays a "we're only friends" game which allows her all the privileges of a love relationship and him none of the advantages. Mme. Tabard also plays with him, but in an amused and tender and ultimately more responsible way, striking a bargain that permits them both satisfaction and leaves neither with a sense of guilt or obligation. Christine calmly manoeuvres her way to a position where she feels that Antoine is ready for her, rewarding him when he behaves with genuine affection, withdrawing when he is boorish or aggressive. Finally, her parents away for the weekend, she puts the television set out of order and summons Antoine to repair it. But this particular relationship is treated with such delicacy and tenderness that we feel that Antoine has matured towards Christine and now deserves her, rather than that he has been tricked or trapped in any way.

Although a consistent pattern emerges of the woman initiating and guiding love affairs, there is no sense that this makes them necessarily unsatisfactory while they last—though the passive and often helpless role of the man is one major reason for the ultimate breakdown which all the affairs, except that of Antoine and Christine, undergo. The characters rarely seem to be able to strike the right balance between submission and control, just as they can neither live completely unaffected by social requirements nor adapt to them. The tensions, satisfactions and failures which Truffaut portrays in sexual relationships are always authentic; he refuses again to sentimentalise, to make things seem easier (or more depressing) than they really are. Along with this goes a refusal to sensationalise or cheapen the quality of love between human beings; his films can be extremely sensual and he was attempting a valid presentation of nudity on the screen (in *Tirez sur le Pianiste*) long before this became safe and fashionable (and one might almost say obligatory), but he never resorts to the slick shorthand of pretending that several acres of bare flesh are an authentic and honest representation of something as complex and mysterious as love. At the heart of all Truffaut's films is a certain chastity, a purity which respects the innocence and mystery and privacy of sex and yet conveys a very physical sense of warmth, desire and tenderness. In *Jules et Jim, Tirez sur le Pianiste* and *Baisers Volés* he has the integrity and honesty to develop the relationships between Catherine and Jim, Charlie and Lena, Antoine and Christine through speech, gesture, movement and touch, to show attraction and misunderstanding and antagonism, and only then to present us, usually very briefly, with the lovers in bed together. This respect for *all* the elements that make up a love relationship also enables him to create an erotic and sensual atmosphere in scenes where the lovers may barely even kiss or touch—such as Mme. Tabard's seduction of Antoine from the other side of his room.

❀     ❀     ❀

Truffaut manages to make both commonplace and extraordinary love affairs take on something of the wonder and freshness of those of adolescence. In an essay on James Dean, written two years before he made *Les Mistons,* he characterises that particular stage of life in this way:

> . . . modesty of feeling, continual fantasy life, moral purity without relation to everyday morality but all the more rigorous, eternal adolescent love of tests and trials, intoxication, pride, and regret at feeling oneself "outside" society, refusal and desire to become integrated and, finally, acceptance—or refusal —of the world as it is.
>
> (*Arts,* September 26, 1956)

These words probably provide the best summing-up of his own films and the reasons for their appeal: characters and themes constantly exemplify this "adolescent" urge to spontaneity, freedom, even anarchy (the influence of Vigo is of course strong) thwarted by or forced to come to terms with society, responsibility, "maturity," "the world as it is." (The word "adolescent" here has of course none of the pejorative connotations that often surround it; it crystallises a stage of life where the tensions between the individual and society are most acute and where most of us begin to make the compromises we spend the rest of our lives regretting.) The elements he defines, transformed into his own films, give them their universality and constant relevance, for they describe a process which we not only all go through but are constantly re-living in various ways.

Behind this concept of adolescence is the traditional contrast of the innocence of childhood and the experience of the adult, except that, like Blake, Truffaut is never sentimental about children and is prepared to make innocence a quality of all who are "childlike," whatever age they may be: Jules, Catherine, Jim, Charlie, Antoine in his twenties, even Montag, all have a childlike naïvety and self-absorption, living "continual fantasy lives" of their own and refusing to accept and sometimes even to understand that the laws which apply to other people affect them too. Even Julie Kohler has a curious childlike quality that survives and perhaps even makes acceptable her cold-blooded murders—she seems determined not so much on revenge as to wipe out some temporary block or interference with the fulfilment of her childhood dream-fantasy of marriage. Once the men are eliminated their action will no longer exist and the marriage can take place after all (as the soaring of the wedding march on the soundtrack at the end indicates). There is something in this of the typical ability of the child to re-mould the world according to his own conception of what it ought to be, and Julie also has the child's refusal to believe anything that doesn't suit the world she has created for herself (such as the fact that the killing of her husband was an accident). The "adolescent" element of the films also helps to account for the sexual modesty and purity that survive even in plots thick with adultery and sexual betrayal: the trio in *Jules et Jim* may behave in a way alien to the formal social law, yet they adhere to their own strict code of honour.

Truffaut is always particularly good at handling children and his first two important films, *Les Mistons* and *Les 400 Coups*, have as the central figures adolescents coming into conflict with the values and demands of the adult world. In the first film the tension between innocence and experience is a psychological one: the boys are growing into sexual maturity but are unable to understand what it is that is happening to them. They relieve their frustrations and bewilderment through violent physical action, noise, half-understood verbal obscenities, yet a certain innocence survives in their idealisation of Bernadette. Their inability to understand and cope with the sexual element in these feelings, however, gives their adoration a mixture of resentful hostility which leads them to follow and persecute her. By the end they have accepted their new condition and are pursuing girls with full awareness of their physical desires, but a certain purity has vanished along with the earlier confusion and bewilderment. The boys still hunt as a gang but are no longer as defiantly outside and apart from society as they were before; a subtle process of assimilation has set in. The film catches beautifully the stage at which innocence and ignorance begin to be transformed into knowledge and experience and reminds us that with a gain in purposefulness and self-confidence there is the loss of something which has vanished even before it could be understood or fully enjoyed, and that much of life will be spent in a vain and only half-conscious attempt to recover this.

Antoine's conflict is more complex and is both psychological and social. He is ambiguously poised between childhood and the adult world; this helps him by enabling him to retreat into

*Preparing the young for the adult world: LES 400 COUPS*

the irresponsibility and freedom of the former at moments of
crisis, but it makes his inevitable return to the standards and
expectations of the adult world tenser each time. Despite his
anti-social tendencies, he has a code of his own by which he
tries to guide his life, but this does not suit the mould into
which society is trying to force him and leads to continual
conflicts. "Society" is not anonymous and faceless; it is made
up of people like those we see in the film who have made
their own compromises in order to achieve a moderate degree
of comfort, the familiarity and security of routine—though they
are constantly, and ironically, under pressure in order to maintain these. They see no reason why Antoine shouldn't do likewise and have no time or inclination to tolerate misfits, and so

they steadily whittle away at him and attempt to make him accept the place assigned him. His case is not exceptional and all the children around him are undergoing the same process to a greater or less degree, although, as long as they remain oblivious to it or resist it, their spontaneity provides a welcome counterbalance to the greyness of the adult world around.

The pervasiveness and irrevocability of this process are vividly illustrated in some of the visual parallels of the film, especially the shot of the three little daughters of one of the reformatory officials being locked up in a cage as soon as the boys are allowed out for a rest period; society both protects and imprisons them, and the shot also recalls that of the three prostitutes in their cell in the police station and hints at what it is that society has to offer the girls. And the freeze-frame of Antoine's face at the end recalls the earlier shots of him being photographed, and hence marked out and labelled for life, in the jail, and brings forcefully home to us the hopelessness of any attempt to escape. The systematic destruction of potentiality is seen in the film as being almost routine; what gives it especial poignancy in this case is Antoine's own nature. Most of the other children have begun to make their own compromises or evasions: some, like the school sneak who goes out of his way to cause Antoine trouble, are already cynical and time-serving; others, like, for all his attractiveness, René, are beginning to strike a "realistic" attitude of compromise and playing along with the system; a few are born outsiders like the shock-haired book-blotter and thief who turns up as the anarchic Fido in Truffaut's next film. Antoine can settle for none of these roles and is neither deceitful, captious nor shrewd enough to avoid the consequences of trying to be true to himself. He has what Truffaut calls both the "refusal and desire to become integrated" and genuinely wants to please his family and even the authorities as far as he can without debasing himself or doing what he realises is cheap and degrading. But society is not prepared to take him on his own terms and it is less overt defiance than his attempts to conform to what he imagines society expects of him (learning his school lessons, taking back the stolen typewriter) which destroy him. The result is an insoluble social conflict as well as a personal tragedy, as the social framework shows itself blindly and perhaps inevitably hostile to the kind of person who could do most to humanise it and give it a vital flexibility and moral honesty.

In *Jules et Jim* the characters seem to have avoided or some-how bypassed the social moulding which trains children to deny their deepest and most spontaneous impulses in order to conform to—and eventually accept as "natural" or "inevitable"—the artificial restrictions which society has to impose on them in order to survive. In the first half of the film they live a child-hood "fantasy life" devoid of rules and obligations except those they have agreed on for themselves. The opening words of the film, spoken by Catherine over a darkened screen, indicate that the tensions of the film will be personal rather than social: "You said to me: I love you. I said to you: wait. I was going to say: take me. You said to me: go away."[2] For most of the film the characters manage to live remarkably free of social ties and pressures, yet the dream world breaks up nevertheless and it becomes difficult under the circumstances to put the blame solely on an alien and restrictive "society." The three have tried to live as though innocence were the *only* element of human experience and have ignored the facts of possessiveness and jealousy, the need for security and stability, which seem to make some sort of social framework and rules necessary. As the fantasy world crumbles, the characters become slightly ridiculous as they try to ignore the reality of what is happening and impose a barrage of letters, appeals and demands on one another in an attempt to keep it intact. Jim in particular has

*Truffaut's BAISERS VOLES. Jean-Pierre Léaud with Harry Max as the detective. Photo: United Artists.*

*On location for FAHRENHEIT 451. Truffaut in peaked cap aboard the fire engine. Photo: Universal.*

*Children: Sabine (Sabine Haudepin) and Catherine in JULES ET JIM*

an impulse both to belong to and stay apart from society which introduces tensions into the relationship and contributes to its failure. The ending finds Jim and Catherine dead and Jules "free," though haunted by the experiences he has gone through, and the narrator's last words bring to the surface the submerged social implications which cannot be avoided for ever: "Catherine had always wished [her ashes] to be scattered to the winds from the top of a hill . . . but it was not allowed." In this film in particular Truffaut manages to fuse together, with honesty, delicacy and emotional vigour, the lure of anarchy, the attraction and joy of a life without external rules and obligations, the inevitable inner pressures which make some sort of accepted standards necessary, and the destructiveness and futility of the rules and conventions we actually have. By refusing to settle for any one of these aspects as the final or self-evident view-point of the film he produces a work of immense complexity, power, suggestiveness and insight.

In other films society is more directly and persistently restrictive or futile. The world of *La Peau Douce* is constructed solely for the impersonal routine of work and business, not for human relationships, with the result that Pierre has to conduct his love affair in hasty, transitory bursts between business commitments and has no chance to allow it to grow and develop. Both he and Nicole are victims of the *specialisation* of modern society which allows them to fulfil one function, and one only, adequately, leaving them to fill in the rest of life as best they can around this. They have grown so used to this that they accept it without much questioning, slipping adroitly into their roles and then letting the role itself control them. Pierre is also a victim of contemporary sexual hypocrisy and his own inhibitions: he cannot face up to the socially unacceptable fact that he wants two women simultaneously and is driven to a series of petty shifts and compromises to avoid coming to terms with this and also to delay making the choice his social conditioning tells him is necessary. Society forces an either/or pattern on him which eliminates the possibility of an honest and rational solution to his problem, and Franca's wholehearted acceptance of the social ethos and the sanctity of marriage, combined with her justifiable rage at his dishonest and devious attempts to evade the issue, ensures that there can be no way out except disaster. Pierre's attempts to gain freedom of manoeuvre are never more than half-hearted, for he is too committed to and entangled in the social framework and its assumptions to be able to act or think independently of them, and his only solution is to regress to a childlike fantasy world where things will work themselves out as long as he takes care not to think about them. But this solution is feasible only when you also have the child's

194

freedom from responsibilities and Pierre has lost that freedom long ago.

The society of *Fahrenheit 451* has pushed even further the process of identifying people with their social roles and has replaced human intimacy by the fake warmth of television "involvement" which spreads its "personalised" affection impartially into millions of homes. Linda shares the already common delusion that television figures are directing all their charm at her alone and is so overcome when "Linda" is asked for her advice that she can't find words to answer. Montag's muttered "There are thousands of Lindas anyway" misses the essential point, which is that *none* of these Lindas is influencing the programme in any way, though *all* are being made to think they are. (A recent contemporary equivalent is a "participation" opera where every so often the action stops and the audience is asked to vote on what should happen next—though the plot blandly continues on its predestined way regardless of the audience's decision.) Integration into "the world as it is" in this film is the equivalent of spiritual death and those of the protagonists who have retained any independence of mind at all are forced to retreat to a world outside society, a world that is deliberately given the naïvety, the clumsiness and the shining pride of early adolescence—though it is an open question as to how long this society can survive, Truffaut's ending being less optimistic than Bradbury's.

Julie Kohler and Charlie Koller both attempt to exist and find their own type of fulfilment outside the social framework. Society is irrelevant as far as Julie is concerned: it has failed to track down her husband's killers and has shown little interest in doing so, and her response is to create a world in which she makes her own laws and is responsible to no one except herself and the dead David. The film gives her an almost magical and childlike freedom to re-mould the external world to suit herself

—she appears to materialise and vanish at will (Truffaut here transforms the mechanical suggestions in the novel of her elusiveness and ability to avoid capture) and seems free of normal restrictions of time and space (she travels over a wide area of Southern France and Switzerland, yet seems to carry out her task in a matter of days, going directly from one victim to the next; in the book the interval between Bliss and Holmes is two years, though all the victims live in the same city). Even the laws of cause and effect seem to be suspended for her—the dying Coral presses the call-bell in his room to summon help, but no one appears and Julie shows not the slightest alarm that anyone will. Here it is the central character who has all the freedom of the adolescent and the ability to make her fantasy life come real, while moral responsibility for her actions is forced back on the audience. Julie shows no sign of guilt or regret for what she does, never comes to terms with society and sits in the police station calmly and dispassionately identifying photographs of her victims in a manner very different from the hysterical triumph of the Julie of the novel. Her freedom is of course illusory; although she has escaped commitment to the values of society, she has created an even more rigid mental and moral trap for herself and is condemned to live in it always.

Charlie too moves through a series of traps, alternately rejecting and trying to integrate himself back into the outside world and finding that he can succeed fully in neither. He experiences three types of social adaptation, each of them unsatisfactory. The anarchic world of his brothers and the gangsters offers a totally illusory freedom, governed by its own rigid codes and mindless vendettas. Fashionable, upper class society as Charlie experiences it during his period of fame as a concert pianist is hollow, self-seeking, basically indifferent to the needs and dignity of the individual. The world he retreats into for most of the film is shabby, sordid and equally self-interested. In all these worlds Charlie is the childlike innocent who never really understands what is going on around him or what the consequences are likely to be until too late. For all his assumed (and occasionally real) toughness and cynicism, he retains a basic modesty and purity of response which can find no counterpart in the world he moves through, and even Lena shows herself capable of a coarseness and viciousness totally alien to him. His escape from society and involvement brings him only loneliness, a kind of spiritual and emotional death; he is incapable of dissociating himself for ever from others and when he is drawn back into the world disaster inevitably follows. Though the terms in which it is presented are different, the dilemma is much the same as that of *Jules et Jim:* involvement in society=responsibility and commitment=taking risks and the danger of failure (especially if one is weak like Charlie); retreat from society=freedom=loneliness and cutting oneself off from the possibility of happiness (and won't succeed anyway).

The attraction of freedom, of escape from the restrictions and confinements of society accounts for much of the joy and spontaneity of Truffaut's films, and in their style and movement, the people and events they create, their freshness and vitality, they convey themselves the "intoxication" which he associates with adolescence. Yet he is also well aware of the inadequacy and futility of attempting to lead a life of perpetual childhood, and of inner and outer needs for stability and commitment. But we give up too much in settling simply for these and making them the be-all and end-all of life and in attempting to disown the adolescent impulses as "childish" or "immature." If we forget them or surrender them completely, the result is to submerge ourselves in routine, sterility, indifference, cynicism, fear of change or novelty or new experiences. The films look from various angles at this basic tension between the freedom of the (spiritual or physical) adolescent and the results of adapting to or attempting to stay apart from social integration. In *Les 400 Coups* childhood potential is carelessly and wastefully destroyed by adults whose own lives are bleak and dissatisfied. In *La Peau Douce* an attempt to move out of the dead and stereotyped routines of contemporary life is destroyed by the nature of an impersonal society and years of unconscious adaptation to its assumptions. *Fahrenheit 451* shows us a totally dead society where individuals have the task of starting again virtually from scratch. The ambiguous relationships between the urge to freedom and the claims of responsibility are presented in *Jules et Jim, Tirez sur le Pianiste* and *La Mariée Etait en Noir*, together with indications of the traps which we create for ourselves even at those times when society seems to have relaxed its hold on us.

Perhaps the most subtle account of the inevitable movement towards integration in society and the consequences of this is *Baisers Volés*. Antoine has freshness, a basic innocence, and youthful impetuousness, but he is also constantly associated with or brought into contact with transience and loneliness (and death—the older detective suddenly and disconcertingly toppling over dead in the middle of a 'phone call). Everything about him is temporary—the places he lives in, the jobs he has, the friends he makes, the girls he makes love to. His life seems constantly to be stopping and then starting again on a slightly different tack, but with nothing ever fundamentally secured or established. His life has much attraction and he is clearly not unhappy in it, but the structure and events of the film constantly equate it with hiding, second-hand experience, dead ends. He is free, certainly, but he is also at the mercy of circumstances, with nothing finally to hold on to or attach himself to. The end sees him accepting, under Christine's gentle but decisive pressure, responsibility and maturity, but with considerable doubt

198

surrounding the probable outcome. Into the delicate and touching proposal scene Truffaut cuts a shot of the stranger waiting patiently outside the gate for Christine to appear, and when the man accosts them outside and insists that it is *he* who is permanent and will never betray her, the result is to give the idea and associations of permanence considerable ambiguity. We are forced to wonder just how long Antoine will succeed in holding down this moment of stability and contentment, and also the implied equation of permanence, faithfulness and loyalty with the stranger's loneliness and stultification (an idea suggested earlier in Antoine's meeting with a now-married former girl friend) makes us consider how much Antoine (and we) might be giving up in return for maturity.

One of Truffaut's greatest strengths as a director is his ability to reveal the limitations and confinements of daily experience in a way which makes us newly aware of and responsive to them. The limitations may be those of personality, habit, routine, stereotyped responses and gestures, the inadequacy of speech, the confinements of place, the needs and demands of other people, the nature and requirements of society and the unconscious adoption of social assumptions as our own and therefore "natural" or "instinctive"—but they are all ways in which our potential for developing as free and complete individuals can be restricted. Against these Truffaut sets up the attraction of the dream, not as a means of escape, but as a way of recovering spontaneity and imagination—qualities linked essentially to childhood and forgotten or discarded in the "realistic" acceptance of maturity. The organisation of the films points to a way of transcending or escaping the unnecessary and arbitrary restrictions of the everyday world, but with a realistic assessment of the limits to which this escape can go and a refusal to surrender to mere fantasy or wish-fulfilment.

Perhaps the most difficult element of Truffaut's films to convey is the blend of sadness and gaiety in all of them. The subjects and characters involve frustration, failure, loneliness and death, and yet the ultimate effect of the films is to make us feel happy —not "feeling good" in the sense that the film-maker has either solved all our problems for us or allowed us to pretend that there aren't really any problems after all, and not suffused in a warm glow of complacency and self-satisfied condescension— but *happy* in a way in which few of us have the chance or allow ourselves to be in ordinary life. He makes us feel life is and can be much richer than we in our own "little circles" ever imagine it to be, and he does this by showing us *all* of it and by making us experience pain, joy, sadness, anger, compassion, frustration, misery and exhilaration in what is suddenly a new and more vital way. He is not an "experimental" film-maker in the sense of innovating wildly new techniques or structures, and he adheres most of the time to what I earlier called "realism" (acknowledging that this is a concept with its own conventions, which change from time to time) and to fairly straightforward plot structures, yet by transforming and re-vitalising these conventions he gives them a new and subversive significance. The films are firmly rooted in the world we all move in and seem to obey its laws, yet the result is to make us profoundly dissatisfied with that world and what we have made out of it. Truffaut's realism is essential for the humanising effect which his films have: we are brought into close emotional involvement with the characters and cannot escape recognising, for good or ill, our own affinity with them, while the style and framework of the films, by releasing us from conventional and stereotyped reactions leads to a freedom normally beyond our grasp, an awareness of and a desire to take in the dimensions of life which we normally ignore.

# 5. Styles: La Sirène du Mississipi

SUSAN SONTAG ARGUES in her essay "On Style"[24] that the traditional critical method of dividing a work of art into "style" and "content" and then attempting to patch the two together into some kind of unity again has rarely been successful and has led instead to a misconception and undervaluing of the whole idea of style. She suggests that it is more useful to look at style as something which contains and shapes or controls other elements such as theme, morality and the artist's personality; that the "mask" of style is in fact the "face" itself. She also makes a useful distinction between "style" and "stylisation," the former being the product of the "will" and the latter of "willfulness." Even the most willful or mannered style, however, is never the result solely of a personal choice or quirk on the part of the artist, for style is something that is also historically conditioned and influenced by the assumptions, values and behaviour of the age the artist lives in.

This last idea has been taken further by Peter Wollen in his book *Signs and Meaning in the Cinema*,[25] where he suggests a fourfold concept of "styles": conscious personal style, unconscious personal style, conscious collective style, and unconscious collective style. The first two of these would combine Sontag's "will" and "willfulness" in varying proportions, conscious personal style being those elements (in a film in this case) of camera technique, theme, attitude to human beings or society as a whole, handling of actors, lighting, music, dialogue and choice of settings or *décor* which can be seen to be characteristic of a particular director and which he seems to be handling purposefully and with full awareness of their nature and implications; while under unconscious personal style would come recurrent images, turns of phrase, obsessive repetitions and ways of handling situations of a particular type which seem to be automatic or conditioned by elements within himself which the artist may not fully understand. Conscious collective style refers to the choices which the artist deliberately makes from among the stylistic alternatives which his culture offers him, and unconscious collective style includes those decisions and limitations which the nature of his culture imposes on him, but of which neither he nor anyone else is fully aware and which can be isolated only in historical perspective. (I am modifying Wollen's definitions in the last two cases for my own purposes.)

I find this classification a very useful one, and it might help to apply it briefly to a well-known literary figure as an illustration of what is involved, before looking at *La Sirène du Mississipi* as an example of Truffaut's "styles." In the mid-Nineteenth century Dickens wrote a series of novels, some of whose main stylistic features are as follows. The books first appeared in the form of monthly or weekly serials and run to an average of seven hundred pages in modern editions. Their plots are intricate and complex, involve and finally draw together dozens of characters and generally end with a restoration of order, a redress of injustice and a happy marriage. The most vivid characters tend to be presented as caricatures with tics of speech and behaviour that impress them firmly on the reader's mind. People are often given the attributes of animals, and places and things are drawn with disturbingly human qualities. The impulse of the books is towards love and charity as regards individuals, but society is presented as more and more corrupt and irredeemable towards the end of Dickens's career. Sentence structure is highly rhetorical and repetitive throughout, but especially so in death-bed scenes and similar crises. Many of the novels centre round the exploitation and mistreatment of small children. Dickens's attitude towards political and social reform veers between liberalism and repression, often in the same book: a genuine sympathy and understanding for the working class co-exists with a fear of the mob and support of "law and order" in the face of revolution. "Snugness," a major element in Dickens's own temperament and one of the chief sources of his appeal to readers, is associated with enclosed spaces and warm fires; on the other hand, he depicts the misery of slums and hovels in terms of enclosure and lack of space, and fire is the destructive weapon of rioters and revolutionaries.

These features could be categorised in the following way (though the categories naturally overlap on occasion). Techniques of characterisation and description are elements of conscious personal style, though features such as the obsessive animal imagery and the merging of animate and inanimate are probably largely unconscious. The rhetorical writing is conscious and controlled, though the tendency to slip into set patterns at moments of emotional crisis is again unconscious and can tell us a great deal about Dickens himself. The concern for exploited and helpless children stems directly from Dickens's own experiences and his time working in a blacking factory as a boy; the theme is one that imposes itself on him time and again without his conscious volition, and responds to psychological needs and urgings of which he was only dimly aware.

The ambivalent attitudes towards fire and space reflect Dickens's own temperament and personality (unconscious personal style) but are also part of a wider and almost universal cultural tradition (unconscious collective style). His political and social attitudes are likewise conditioned both by his own inner needs and fears and by the predominant attitudes and events in the society of his time. The impulse towards love and forgiveness is conscious and personal, but the gradual disillusionment with society seems to find expression in the novels before Dickens was fully aware of it himself and is of course directly related to what was going on in Victorian society. The choice of the novel form and serial publication are conscious and collective, in the sense that the drama and the essay were possible alternatives, but they reflect also the pattern of Victorian reading taste and publishing methods and the assumptions about length and subject-matter to which a writer had to conform to gain an audience. And the structure of the novels, in their complexity and final resolution, reflects assumptions about the nature of human experience which the Victorians took for granted but which are largely alien to the modern reader. The novels follow a pattern of cause and development, coherence, and final explanation which reflect perfectly the views which the Nineteenth century wished to hold about life as a whole; they are self-contained and leave no loose ends for the reader to worry over or interpret for himself. For all the acuteness and virulence with which Dickens dissects contemporary society, the form of the novels breathes a security and harmony which, in the circumstances, was quite unavoidable and of which he was probably totally unaware. In this respect it was quite impossible for him to write in any other way than he did; an open-ended, fragmentary, inconclusive, "do-it-yourself" novel was literally unthinkable for him.

*　　*　　*

An application of these categories to Truffaut's films might help towards an understanding of what "style" involves in the cinema. *La Sirène du Mississipi* seems to be a resting-place in his career to date; it provides an almost ideal synthesis of every feature of his style and is full of echoes, many of them deliberate, of his earlier films. As the film may not have received wide distribution at the time this book appears, a brief summary of the plot may be useful.

*LA SIRENE DU MISSISSIPI: the detective Comolli (Michel Bouquet, at left) and Louis (Jean-Paul Belmondo)*

Louis Mahe, the wealthy owner of a tobacco factory on the island of Réunion, has arranged a marriage by correspondence with a girl whom he has seen only in a photograph. The girl he is expecting does not arrive on the steamer *Mississipi,* but another, much more beautiful girl, manages to convince him that she is the Julie Roussel he is to marry. The wedding takes place and they are blissfully happy for some time, though some of the girl's actions puzzle him and seem inconsistent with the information she had given him about herself by letter. One day Julie vanishes, taking with her almost all the money in their joint bank accounts. Louis is told by Berthe Roussel that the girl he married is not her sister, and the two of them hire a private detective to track down the false Julie and discover if there has been any foul play. Louis also takes up the search himself and, after a short bout of illness, finds Julie working as a night club hostess in the South of France. He gives up his intention of killing her on discovering that he is still in love with her, and she convinces him that she was forced to do what she did by an accomplice who had murdered the original Julie. They set up house again together in Aix-en-Provence, but Louis one day encounters the detective, still on Julie's trail. He tells him to give up the search, but the detective says he is still in Berthe's employ and has a duty towards her. He follows Louis back home, and in desperation Louis kills him. The lovers flee to Lyon, but the girl's expensive tastes force Louis to sell his factory to keep them in funds. The detective's body is discovered; Louis and Julie (whose real name is Marion) escape from the police but have to leave all their money behind. They hide out in an abandoned shack in the Swiss Alps and Julie/Marion begins slowly to poison Louis. He discovers what she is doing, but his love for her enables him to forgive her. His generosity shames her and makes her fully aware of her own deep love for him, and the two decide to face the future together.

In almost every respect the "conscious personal style" of the film is typical of Truffaut. The credits have behind them a confusing babble of voices reading out marriage advertisements from a newspaper column and the opening sequences are constructed in a series of hints, allusions and mysteries which draw the viewer into the film and leave him to puzzle out relationships for himself. Then once the viewer has congratulated himself on solving the "mystery" of Julie/Marion,* Truffaut switches

---

*I will call her Marion throughout, to avoid confusion with Julie Kohler of *La Mariée Etait en Noir*.

focus, problems of pursuit and discovery fall into the background and the emphasis is placed on the complex sequence of trust, betrayal and reconciliation between the lovers. The process is similar to that in Hitchcock's *Vertigo* or in *La Mariée Etait en Noir*, and a clue is provided by a visit which Louis and Marion make to see *Johnny Guitar* in the course of the film. She expresses surprise that it isn't a "shoot-'em-up" Western, and he explains that it's a "story of the emotions." One recurring feature of Truffaut's films is the desire to dislocate the traditional *genres*, especially the detective story, and to make the audience experience a pattern of emotions totally different to that which they are expecting.

There is less emphasis then on whether Louis and Marion are going to be caught than on whether they can come to terms with and understand each other. Each has committed or been accomplice to a murder, but moral judgements are suspended while the film investigates human inter-relationships. The fluidity and serenity of the camera style allow for a slackening of tension and permit the emotional situation to work itself out within a framework that provides little sense of urgency. Moments of quick cutting during the scenes on Réunion help to create the suspense necessary at this stage (the series of shots which establish that there is something mysterious about Marion's behaviour), but in general this part of the film is shot in a series of long takes which allow us to savour the richness and visual beauty of the setting and create a rhythm and atmosphere that make ideas of murder and theft seem totally out of place. The scene in which Louis discovers Marion's betrayal is slow and cumulative, the final confirmation of suspicions he had held for some time and refused to admit: from the verandah of the house the camera watches him arrive home at nightfall and search the garden, calling for her; he enters the house and the camera waits till he appears on the verandah; he vanishes into

*Louis searches "Julie's" trunk and discovers her deception in LA SIRENE DU MISSISSIPI*

the rooms there, re-appears and finally opens the trunk she had brought with her to discover belongings that could not possibly be hers—all in one take. The camera in this section of the film is constantly creative, almost always on the move, adjusting to the characters and expressing emotions with little need of dialogue or explanation. Louis's rage and grief at Marion's betrayal are conveyed in a sequence that begins with a close-up of an open fire into which her underclothes are being hurled; cuts show this scene from several angles, yet give the impression of a steady zoom in; then there is a cut to a medium-shot that takes in Louis's arm (the most we see of him in the scene); the camera tracks in from this and the music ends to leave only the crackling of the flames.

During the scenes on Réunion the screen is visually packed, either with the beauties of the natural landscape and the lushness of the huge garden of Louis's house, or filled with people, as when the camera zooms back from a shot of Louis and Marion on the church steps after their wedding to take in the huge crowd waiting to greet them. The setting is all but that of a dream landscape and Truffaut concentrates almost entirely on exteriors—little attention is paid to details of furnishings and we hardly see the inside of the house at any length at all (except for one beautifully subtle shot of Louis and Marion together in bed at night which begins in almost complete darkness and then lights up very slowly as though our eyes were accustoming

*LA SIRENE DU MISSISSIPI: Marion (Catherine Deneuve) and Louis are married*

themselves to the dark). The effect is to set up the typical tension between a happiness that is private, self-contained, dream-like and temporary, and the realities of a world of more complex emotions, of suffering and betrayal.

After the move to France, although the rhythm of the film remains fairly constant (another very long take, for example, is when the camera tracks to follow Marion as she comes out of her hotel and crosses the street to the night club where she works, then watches Louis enter the frame, follows him as he goes to the night club and then back to the hotel, and pans and tilts with him as he climbs up the fire-escape to her room), the focus is drastically narrowed. We see virtually nothing of the landscape apart from a long-shot of Lyon and some shots

*Louis makes his way to Marion's hotel room*

of the scenery round the shack at the end, and the only interior shown at length is that of their flat in Lyon, which has virtually no furniture and no decorations or ornaments and consists simply of bare whitewashed walls with mysterious pencilled scribbles over them. The various car journeys are shot largely in close-up, as opposed to the long-shots of the corresponding scenes on Réunion. The effect is that of a closed environment within which the couple will have to come to terms with themselves before they can find the freedom they are seeking and virtually no other characters appear in this part of the film, except for the detective, a landlady, and Louis's business partner Jardine.

The obstacles to their freedom, the traps into which they blunder and from which they have to extricate themselves are largely self-created. Once again the woman is the dominant partner, taking the initiative, creating and controlling the nature of the relationship. The man is weak, gullible, but fundamentally generous, and it is his generosity which enables Marion to overcome the self-interest that is her dominant motivation, though it is clear that it will always be in her power to continue or end their reconciliation and the film as usual leaves us with no final resolution. Marion, however, is less convincing than most of Truffaut's other women—not through any weakness in Catherine Deneuve's performance, which creates particularly well the mixture of wary experience and frivolity within the character—but because the division of interest between herself and Louis does not allow the complexity of her character to be fully realised. Her shifts of position towards Louis, especially at the end, seem rather too arbitrary and Truffaut has to allow her to explain herself verbally far more than usual in an attempt to counter this. The impulse towards reconciliation is evident throughout the film, however, from the opening clip from Renoir's *La Marseillaise* and the place name Réunion onwards, and the end of the film simply ignores traditional moral categories of guilt and punishment and leaves the characters trudging off in the snow towards whatever destiny awaits them.

Louis and Marion have been forced to come to terms with the balance between joy and suffering in human experience and to accept each other for the fallible, untrustworthy creatures they are. Marion is no longer for Louis the materialisation of an impossible ideal, nor can she be placed simply in the category of liar and murderess by the audience. The ending, however, introduces a complexity of tone missing from most of the remainder of the film. There are moments of exhilaration and gaiety and the physical joy of love is vividly conveyed (rarely in conventional fashion—Marion strips to the waist, not in the bedroom but standing in their beautiful red car in the middle of a country road, causing a passing motorist to swerve his beautiful blue car off the road and into a tree as he gazes at her), but until the scenes in the Alps there are few of the disconcerting juxtapositions of other films. As Louis and Marion discover the abandoned shack (the same one which Charlie and his brothers use as a hide-out in *Tirez sur le Pianiste*) Marion mutters that it would be a good place to end a gangster film in; Louis recklessly scatters mounds of poison all over the floor to discourage rats, giving his wife an inspiration as to how to dispose of him; and the final shots of Marion in a ludicrous black sable and ostrich-feather coat walking away with him across the snow have something of the absurdity of Marlene Dietrich tottering on high heels into the desert after Gary Cooper at the end of *Morocco*.

Truffaut then is consciously both exploiting and varying resources, techniques and themes which are evident in his earlier

*Opposite: Louis reads Balzac while Marion meditates on rat poison (above), and (below) a moment of tenderness between them*

212

films. Clothes and settings are used aesthetically and thematically, though without the minute attention to detail evident in
William Irish's novel.[17] Music is more dominant than in recent
films, though it is still reserved mainly for bursts of physical
activity or to accentuate moments of tension—with silence again
accompanying scenes of emotional depth, such as that in which
Louis and Marion sit by the fire in their house in Aix. Major
elements of theme and camera technique form part of a style
which, for all its variety, is recognisably that of Truffaut and
no one else.

Yet though repetition may be (as Susan Sontag suggests) an
essential element of any style, and though it may be useful to
trace recurring thematic or stylistic patterns in the work of any
artist, the mere fact that a particular work falls neatly into its
allotted place does not necessarily guarantee its quality. The
repetition of techniques and motifs may testify to the determination of an artist to mould the world to his own particular
vision of it, but it can equally well become automatic, a sign
of an imagination not working at full pressure and allowing
something to slip by simply because it worked well before—a
process that may be purely unconscious.

I don't think *La Sirène du Mississipi* is by any means a bad
film, but its very real weaknesses seem to be attributable to
this aspect of Truffaut's "unconscious personal style," his allowing certain situations to fall into patterns which come very
easily to him, but which may not be entirely appropriate or
desirable. (Unconscious personal style can also, of course, as
in Dickens, be a source of strength.) In almost every instance
where this happens the situation is one of crisis or heightened
intensity in the love relationship and this hints at a fundamental
uncertainty on Truffaut's part as to how to handle it. Once
again he follows the original novel very closely for nine-tenths
of its length (allowing for the changes in time and place—

214

updating it from the 1880s to the present day and setting it in Réunion and France instead of Louisiana and Florida), and the only drastic change comes in the ending: in Irish's book the girl repents of the poisoning too late, Louis eventually dies and she is left expecting imminent arrest. His characteristic generosity towards his people, however, leads him to soften the character of Marion and make her much less calculatingly vicious and amoral than the Julia/Bonny of the book; Marion is frivolous with a core of hardness, but much more genuinely attached to Louis throughout than her counterpart in the novel. The result is that the weakness of the novel is exactly reversed: Truffaut creates a sense of genuine love and tenderness between

*Marion discovers the body of Comolli in LA SIRENE DU MISSISSIPI*

his characters which makes Marion's attempt to poison Louis rather difficult to take, while Irish presents a near-degenerate "with no moral sense at all" who is perfectly capable of poisoning her husband but less so of repenting.

The difficulties and uncertainties entailed by this are vividly reflected in the way in which moments of emotional crisis are handled in the film. When Louis discovers Marion and threatens to kill her, she confesses her guilt and tries to justify herself by telling him about her past life. The scene is shot in exactly the same manner as Theresa's confession to Charlie in *Tirez sur le Pianiste*, with the girl pacing restlessly to and fro as she talks and the camera panning constantly with her; brief close-ups of the listening man are intercut with this and snatches of music are heard behind the dialogue. Towards the end the final reconciliation of the lovers is shot largely in long held close-ups of their faces as they embrace—just like the scene between Jules and Catherine in *Jules et Jim*. When Louis returns from Réunion after selling the factory he finds Marion apparently asleep on the bed. His fundamental insecurity about their relationship is conveyed in the way in which, like Pierre of *La Peau Douce*, he kneels and gently strokes her sleeping body. When he first meets Marion, she seems to materialise wraith-like beside his car, like Julie of *La Mariée Etait en Noir*. During his illness, his dreams are presented in the same way as those of Montag in *Fahrenheit 451*, by repeated images of fast tracking shots of trees, roads and railway lines, superimposed one on top of the other. (Curiously, when describing his dreams to a nurse he gives a totally different account and says that they were of a woman dressed in white standing in the middle of the road.) Louis nerves himself for an encounter by talking to his reflection in the mirror, like Antoine in *Baisers Volés*.

Some of these echoes, such as the last, are clearly deliberate, but the fact that there are so many of them seems to indicate that Truffaut, not fully at ease with the situations and characters he has created, has unconsciously turned to methods which succeeded in the past in the hope that they will be enough in themselves to make the scenes convincing. Certainly few members of any audience will recognise or care about these repetitions, but they stem from a failure to re-think technique in terms of the particular relationships involved and so ensure that most of these scenes will appear subtly unsatisfactory.

*     *     *

It is a commonplace that the contemporary arts display a greater variety of potential styles than those of almost any other period. There seem no longer to be any rules or restrictions; the artist seems free to experiment and innovate endlessly, with the only criterion that of acceptance by critics and public. Yet this apparent freedom is nevertheless curtailed by assumptions and expectations to which we are still too close to be able clearly to isolate or identify. It is difficult today, for example, to find a serious painter who would consent to do a landscape, a poet prepared to launch a blank verse epic, or a novelist at ease with the omniscient author technique. The limitations are still there; it is just that they stem from moral, social and political assumptions which we take so much for granted that we genuinely find it impossible to believe that a serious artist should wish to, or be able to deviate from them.

The contemporary film-maker, working in a relatively young art, has more freedom than most, but is still forced to make a choice among stylistic possibilities of which he is consciously aware, and is equally the prisoner of moral assumptions, technical preconceptions and financial limitations which may be so instinctive as to be unrecognisable.

Truffaut has consistently expressed his desire to be a genuinely popular director; he wants people to come and see his films and is unhappy when they don't. This differentiates him immediately not only from directors like Bresson and Godard who appear to be genuinely indifferent to the degree of popular success their films achieve, but also from men like Resnais and Antonioni who want to find an audience but are reluctant to make any concessions towards it. It also brings him into conflict with what is still a predominant critical assumption (and not just in the cinema): that the best works of art are generally those that make fewest concessions to their audience and have therefore to make their way in the face of neglect or hostility. Such critics may find themselves forced to like and even admire Truffaut, but they will instinctively place him on a lower level of achievement than Godard or Resnais and will find their suspicions confirmed when a film like *La Mariée Etait en Noir,* which they see (which they *have* to see) as a glossy and trivial diversion, is one of the biggest money-makers in Paris in 1968.

Truffaut's desire to reach a wide audience means that he has had consciously to accept, in three of his last four films at least, those elements of contemporary cinema which audiences and producers demand almost by instinct: colour, wide-screen or Cinemascope, exotic and glamorous settings, star names in the leading roles, and expensive clothes, houses, furniture and cars. (*Baisers Volés,* on the other hand, dispenses with almost all of these except colour.) A film-maker of Truffaut's integrity can then do one or both of two things: he can accept all these and use them for his own purposes, or he can accept them as an inescapable necessity and a guarantee of minimum success and then proceed to choose from among the available contemporary collective styles those which suit his own temperament whether or not they have much popular appeal.

Some of the choices of this kind open to him can be described as follows. He can produce a film that is fragmentary and arbitrary (reflecting current assumptions about the nature of human experience) or he can attempt to impose a definite shape and pattern on his material. He can choose between something close to traditional narrative structure or something apparently disjointed and inconclusive. He can opt for characters who are "true-to-life" and "realistic" or figures who are symbolic, metaphorical or wildly non-realistic. He can express himself in terms mainly of visual images or of words and dialogue. He can accept, modify or reject the current freedom in the treatment of nudity and sexual behaviour. He can attempt to entertain his audience or to insult, shock or deliberately bore them. He can adopt a visual style that depends mainly on editing or one that relies on *mise en scène* and within this framework he can adopt devices such as elaborate zooms, colour filters and switches of focus for lyrical effect, or he can select a plainer less obtrusive style of filming.

These elements are not mutually exclusive but it is possible to find a considerable degree of consistency in the choices Truffaut makes. His films generally follow a coherent progress towards some kind of resolution, yet they are also open-ended and reflect the inconclusiveness of everyday experience. His use of something close to a conventional narrative structure (however fragmented and episodic it may sometimes be) allows him to engage and then subvert the expectations of his audience (arguably a more effective and useful procedure than deliberately confusing and alienating them from the start). The influence of his mentor André Bazin can be seen in his adoption of what is basically *mise en scène* enabling him to give his films their characteristic fluidity and rhythmic progression; when specific technical devices are employed they almost invariably have a definite purpose and function and are not those which simply give the film a spuriously modish aura. Human beings are presented in a way that brings them vividly to life; they

219

are treated with compassion and generosity, so that we can see in them our own strengths and defects. Sex is accepted as a normal part of human experience, but the focus is placed as firmly on emotional relationships as on physical attraction. *La Sirène du Mississipi* is an almost perfect compendium of all these.

These choices within the framework of collective style are not arbitrary; they reflect and are conditioned by Truffaut's own temperament, his "personal style." They result in films which are graceful, vital, stimulating; they attract by their honesty and their accessibility, and at the same time as they attract they disconcert, impelling us towards a more generous and perceptive assessment of the world around us.

*       *       *

Behind those elements of collective style of which the artist can reasonably be assumed to be conscious lurks a more nebulous and pervasive area within which no one can hope to free himself entirely. Elements mentioned earlier, such as colour, the use of expensive clothes and cars, and the need to have attractive, preferably young people in the central roles, fall partly into this category as well. They take their place in a system of signs recognisable to both the producers and consumers of mass entertainment, the means by which the film industry plays its part in limiting and conditioning the desires and wants of its audience. In the world created by cinema of this kind people are eternally young and beautiful, their houses are spacious and exquisitely furnished even when they are supposed to be struggling to make ends meet, princesses, secretaries and girls existing on the brink of poverty all wear clothes designed by Cardin, and slums and dingy back streets are photographed so as to look romantic and desirable. There is a whole set of mutually accepted signs of this kind around the subject of cars for example: they have to be brightly coloured and preferably convertibles; they have a homing instinct for parking spots, even in the centre of London, Paris or New York, only a yard away from where the character wants to go to; and no one ever bothers to wear a seat-belt while driving them or to lock them when they get out (almost the only exception to this that I can think of is *Bullitt*—where the hero is a police-man). These examples may appear trivial, but adherence to the conventions implied in them can give an air of falsity to the most doggedly authentic films.

In some cases, like *Tirez sur le Pianiste, Les 400 Coups*, and *Baisers Volés*, Truffaut simply ignores most of these, but *La Sirène du Mississipi* seems on the surface to fall into every trap possible. Louis Mahe, for example, a slightly paunchy thirty-seven-year old in the book, acutely conscious of his age and his lack of sexual attractiveness, is incarnated in Jean-Paul Bel-mondo. Both he and Marion wear gorgeously designed clothes all through the film, even when they are supposed to be down to their last ten francs, and drive around in a red convertible. And the Réunion settings in particular convey an almost over-powering atmosphere of luxury and beauty. It would seem easy to indict Truffaut for yielding to the temptation to glamorise and falsify his material; one could go further and accuse him of joining those forces in the contemporary cinema whose energies are devoted to the creation and satisfaction of the most spurious and banal wants in their audience, thus distracting them from thinking or caring about more vital problems.

Condemnation along these lines, however, would imply that the only type of cinema which can be intellectually honest is that which rigidly eschews stars and exoticism of any kind and that any film which deliberately aims at attracting a wide audi-ence is automatically forced to make so many concessions as

*Louis and Marion in the garden of their house on Réunion . . .*

to become worthless. For Truffaut, while ostensibly adopting the formulae of mass cinema, is busy turning them to his own purposes and even subverting them. It is not so much greed (as in Irish's novel) as the more contemporary vice of a mania for useless and conspicuous luxury which is the driving impulse behind Marion and which leads her to the brink of destroying both herself and Louis. She wants constantly to live both beyond her needs and her means and is totally indifferent as to the methods by which her wants are satisfied and the consequences these entail. The disparity between her compulsive acquisition of more and more luxurious and useless clothing and the barrenness of the life they are leading (aptly symbolised by their flat

*. . . and Marion in her luxurious coat sets off with Louis
at the end of LA SIRENE DU MISSISSIPI*

in Lyon) becomes steadily more absurd and culminates in the
spectacle of her ploughing her way through the snow at the
end dressed in a coat which she has confessed to Louis even
Parisians would find rather ridiculous. *La Sirène du Mississipi*,
like *La Mariée Etait en Noir*, seems to indicate that Truffaut,
more than any other contemporary director, is capable of creating a cinema which is both popular and subversive.

Other features of "unconscious collective style" can be more
briefly noted. They include conventions in the manner of presenting information to the audience: factual information must
be given visually whenever possible—so the suspicions of both
Louis and the audience that Marion is poisoning him are

aroused by his fortuitous glimpsing of a cartoon sequence in a newspaper of Snow White eating the poisoned apple. At the beginning of the film the audience is given privileged information about Marion that allows them to suspect her long before Louis does (and thus feel superior to him), in accordance with well-established formulae: the first three clues (the wedding ring that doesn't fit her finger, her drinking coffee when she is supposed not to like it, and her indifference to the death of her pet bird) are made available to character and audience simultaneously, but her slipping out of the house to meet her accomplice (emphasised by her being masked off in a corner of the screen at the beginning of the shot, and by appropriately portentous music) is revealed only to the audience.

*Louis finds that the wedding ring doesn't fit his bride's finger*

There are also wider collective assumptions to which any serious artist in the mid-Twentieth century must almost instinctively adhere. In contrast to the Nineteenth century desire for works of art which present a coherent and stable interpretation of life and suggest that most problems are soluble, or at least explicable, the contemporary framework within which Truffaut works assumes that final resolutions and explanations are false and unrealistic, and a film that wraps up its loose ends too neatly becomes automatically suspect. It is equally impossible today to conceive of a hero in the Nineteenth century manner; that too is now "unrealistic" and the central figure must show himself to be fallible and insecure if he is to convince. (Stylised forms such as the epic and the Western used to be able to continue the tradition of the hero undisturbed, but even they are now moving towards anti-heroes and non-heroes.) The typical modern "hero" is isolated and lonely, cut off from traditional values and unable to find satisfaction in taking his place within a stable social framework or in political action. The only consolation left is "love" and any work that does not centre itself round the sexual relationship as the most important personal factor in contemporary experience is setting up barriers to public acceptance from the start.

Aspects of all these can be discerned in *La Sirène du Mississipi* as in all of Truffaut's other films. Obviously they interact to a considerable extent with his "personal style," but it would be rash to claim that his fondness for open-ended films, centering round the misfortunes of a weak, wrong-headed or unfortunate character, showing a distinct hostility or indifference to organised society, and with love and personal relationships providing the chief positive values, is the result purely of his own temperament.

Behind these easily recognisable elements of collective style are others not so obvious, such as the prevalent and unspoken assumption that people and events of past ages are interesting only in so far as they can be re-interpreted and assimilated to the concerns and interests of the present day—a preconception which may have played its part in the updating of *La Sirène du Mississipi* just as much as the difficulties which filming a subject from the late Nineteenth century in a convincing setting would have presented a director like Truffaut who likes to work on location and as authentically as possible.

❋　❋　❋

*Jean-Pierre Cargol as the "wild boy" in*
*L'ENFANT SAUVAGE*

If *La Sirène du Mississipi* represents the tendency in Truffaut's work to accept and utilise the paraphernalia of film-making for a mass audience in the Sixties, the picture which he has just finished, *L'Enfant Sauvage*, indicates a return to the more private world of *Les 400 Coups* or *Tirez sur le Pianiste*. Set at the very end of the Eighteenth century, it is based on the true account of the attempts of a French doctor to reclaim and civilise a "wild boy" who had spent his whole childhood living like an animal in the woods. There will be few, if any, star names in it (Truffaut himself taking the role of the doctor) and the fact that the action takes place largely indoors or in the countryside should allow for the period authenticity impossible in the city settings of *La Sirène du Mississipi*. The emphasis of the scenario is clearly on one of Truffaut's favourite themes—the conflict between individual freedom and the consequences and implications of social adaptation, the boy's acceptance of love and security going hand-in-hand with the literal loss of his ability to exist on his own. After *L'Enfant Sauvage* he plans another chapter in the saga of Antoine Doinel; there should be good times ahead.

# Filmography

*FILMS DIRECTED BY TRUFFAUT*
UNE VISITE. 1955. (16mm short). *Photography:* Jacques
Rivette. *Editor:* Alain Resnais.
LES MISTONS (THE MISCHIEF-MAKERS). 1958. *Screen-play:* François Truffaut. *Based on the short story* Virginales
*by:* Maurice Pons. *Photography:* Jean Maligo. *Editor:* Cécile
Decugis. *Music:* Maurice Le Roux. *Commentary spoken by:*
Michel François. *Production:* Les Films du Carrosse. 2,340 feet.
26 minutes.
  *Players:* Bernadette Lafont *(Bernadette)*, Gérard Blain *(Gé-rard)*.
HISTOIRE D'EAU. 1959. *Co-Director:* Jean-Luc Godard. *Pho-tography:* Michel Latouche. *Production:* Les Films de la Pléiade.
20 minutes.

LES QUATRE CENTS COUPS (THE 400 BLOWS). 1959.
*Screenplay:* François Truffaut. *Dialogue:* Marcel Moussy. *Story:*
François Truffaut. *Photography* (Dyaliscope): Henri Decae. *Art
Director:* Bernard Evein. *Editor:* Marie-Josèphe Yoyotte. *Music:*
Jean Constantin. *Sound:* Jean-Claude Marchetti. *Production:* Les
Films du Carrosse/SEDIF. 8,460 feet. 94 minutes.
  *Players:* Jean-Pierre Léaud *(Antoine Doinel)*, Claire Maurier
*(His mother)*, Albert Rémy *(His father)*, Guy Decomble *(School-master)*, Patrick Auffay *(René)*, Georges Flamant *(René's fa-ther)*, Daniel Couturier, François Nocher, Richard Kanayan
*(Children)*. *Special guest appearance by:* Jeanne Moreau *(Wom-an in street with dog)*, Jean-Claude Brialy *(Man in street)*.

*Opposite: Charlie and Lena in TIREZ SUR LE PIANISTE*

TIREZ SUR LE PIANISTE (SHOOT THE PIANIST, SHOOT THE PIANO-PLAYER). 1960. *Screenplay:* François Truffaut, Marcel Moussy. *Dialogue:* François Truffaut. *Based on the novel* Down There *by:* David Goodis. *Photography* (Dyaliscope): Raoul Coutard. *Art Director:* Jacques Mely. *Editor:* Claudine Bouche. *Music:* Jean Constantin. *Song* "Dialogues d'amoureux" *composed and sung by:* Felix Leclerc and Lucianne Vernay. *Song* "Framboise" *by:* Boby Lapointe. *Sound:* Jacques Gallois. *Producer:* Pierre Braunberger. *Production:* Les Films de la Pléiade. 7,200 feet. 80 minutes.

*Players:* Charles Aznavour *(Charlie Koller/Edouard Saroyan)*, Nicole Berger *(Theresa)*, Marie Dubois *(Lena)*, Michèle Mercier *(Clarisse)*, Albert Rémy *(Chico Saroyan)*, Claude Mansard *(Momo)*, Daniel Boulanger *(Ernest)*, Richard Kanayan *(Fido Saroyan)*, Jacques Aslanian *(Richard Saroyan)*, Serge Davri *(Plyne)*, Claude Heymann *(Lars Schmeel)*.

JULES ET JIM (JULES AND JIM). 1961. *Screenplay:* François Truffaut, Jean Gruault. *Based on the novel by:* Henri-Pierre Roché. *Photography* (Franscope): Raoul Coutard. *Editor:* Claudine Bouche. *Music:* Georges Delerue. *Song* "Le Tourbillon" *by:* Bassiak. *Sound:* Temoin. *Production:* Les Films du Carrosse/ SEDIF. 9,450 feet. 105 minutes.

*Players:* Jeanne Moreau *(Catherine)*, Oskar Werner *(Jules)*, Henri Serre *(Jim)*, Marie Dubois *(Thérèse)*, Vanna Urbino *(Gilberte)*, Sabine Haudepin *(Sabine)*, Boris Bassiak *(Albert)*, Jean-Louis Richard *(1st customer in café)*, Michel Varesano *(2nd customer in café)*, Pierre Fabre *(Drunkard in café)*, Danielle Bassiak *(Albert's friend)*, Bernard Largemains *(Merlin)*, Elen Bober *(Mathilde)*, Michel Subor *(Narrator)*.

> *Opposite: the first meeting between Catherine and Jules and Jim (above); Antoine's father offers him his lighter to burn the place down properly after the boy has been caught reading Balzac (below)*

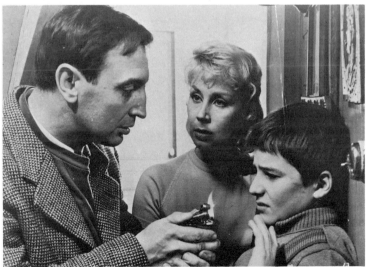

ANTOINE ET COLETTE (Episode in the compilation film L'AMOUR A VINGT ANS—LOVE AT TWENTY). 1962. *Screenplay:* François Truffaut. *Dialogue:* Yvon Samuel. *Photography:* (Cinemascope): Raoul Coutard. *Editor:* Claudine Bouche. *Linking Music:* Georges Delerue. *Producer:* Pierre Rostang. *Production:* Ulysse-Unitec.

*Players:* Jean-Pierre Léaud *(Antoine Doinel)*, Marie-France Pisier *(Colette)*, François Darbon *(Colette's father)*, Rosy Varte *(Colette's mother)*.


LA PEAU DOUCE (SOFT SKIN, SILKEN SKIN). 1964. *Screenplay:* François Truffaut, Jean-Louis Richard. *Photography:* Raoul Coutard. *Editor:* Claudine Bouche. *Music:* Georges Delerue. *Production:* Les Films du Carrosse/SEDIF. 10,635 feet. 118 minutes.

*Players:* Jean Desailly *(Pierre Lachenay)*, Françoise Dorléac *(Nicole Chomette)*, Nelly Bénédetti *(Franca Lachenay)*, Daniel Ceccaldi *(Clément)*, Laurence Badie *(Ingrid)*, Jean Lanier *(Michel)*, Paule Emanuele *(Odile)*, Philippe Dumat *(Cinema manager)*, Pierre Risch *(Canon)*, Dominique Lacarrière *(Pierre's secretary)*, Sabine Haudepin *(Sabine)*, Maurice Garrel *(Bookseller)*, Gerard Poirot *(Franck)*, Georges de Givray *(Nicole's father)*, Charles Lavialle *(Hotel night-porter)*, Carnero *(Lisbon organiser)*, Catherine Duport *(Young girl at Reims dinner)*.


FAHRENHEIT 451. 1966. *Screenplay:* François Truffaut, Jean-Louis Richard. *Based on the novel by:* Ray Bradbury. *Additional dialogue:* David Rudkin, Helen Scott. *Photography* (Technicolor): Nicolas Roeg. *Art Director:* Syd Cain. *Design and costume consultant:* Tony Walton. *Special effects:* Bowie Films,

*Opposite: the Captain, Montag and the fire engine in*
*FAHRENHEIT 451*

Rank Films Processing Division, Charles Staffel. *Editor:* Thom Noble. *Music:* Bernard Herrmann. *Sound:* Norman Wanstall. *Producer:* Lewis M. Allen. *Production:* Anglo-Enterprise/Vineyard. 10,080 feet. 112 minutes.

*Players:* Oskar Werner *(Montag)*, Julie Christie *(Linda Montag/Clarisse)*, Cyril Cusack *(The Captain)*, Anton Diffring *(Fabian)*, Jeremy Spenser *(Man with the apple)*, Bee Duffell *(The Book-Woman)*, Gillian Lewis *(TV announcer)*, Ann Bell *(Doris)*, Caroline Hunt *(Helen)*, Anna Palk *(Jackie)*, Roma Milne *(Neighbour)*, Alex Scott *(The Life of Henry Brulard)*, Dennis Gilmore *(Martian Chronicles)*, Fred Cox *(Pride)*, Frank Cox *(Prejudice)*,

*LA MARIEE ETAIT EN NOIR: Julie discovers Fergus's painting of her (and his love for her) after killing him*

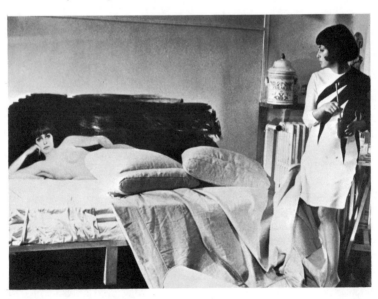

Michael Balfour *(Machiavelli's Prince)*, Judith Drynan *(Plato's Dialogues)*, David Glover *(The Pickwick Papers)*, Yvonne Blake *(The Jewish Question)*, John Rae *(Weir of Hermiston)*, Earl Younger *(Nephew of Weir of Hermiston)*, Arthur Cox *(1st male nurse)*, Eric Mason *(2nd male nurse)*, Noel Davis and Donald Pickering *(TV announcers)*, Michael Mundell *(Stoneman)*, Chris Williams *(Black)*, Gillian Aldam *(Judoka woman)*, Edward Kaye *(Judoka man)*, Mark Lester *(1st small boy)*, Kevin Elder *(2nd small boy)*, Joan Francis *(Bar telephonist)*, Tom Watson *(Sergeant instructor)*.

LA MARIEE ETAIT EN NOIR (THE BRIDE WORE BLACK). 1968. *Screenplay:* François Truffaut, Jean-Louis Richard. *Based on the novel* The Bride Wore Black *by:* Cornell Woolrich. *Photography* (Eastman Colour): Raoul Coutard. *Art Director:* Pierre Guffroy. *Editor:* Claudine Bouche. *Music:* Bernard Herrmann. *Sound:* René Levert. *Producer:* Marcel Roberts. *Production:* Les Films du Carrosse/Artistes Associés (Paris)/ Dino de Laurentiis Cinematografica (Rome). 9,672 feet. 107 minutes.

*Players:* Jeanne Moreau *(Julie Kohler)*, Jean-Claude Brialy *(Corey)*, Michel Bouquet *(Robert Coral)*, Charles Denner *(Fergus)*, Claude Rich *(Bliss)*, Daniel Boulanger *(Delvaux)*, Michel Lonsdale *(Clément Morane)*, Serge Rousseau *(David)*, Jacques Robiolles *(Charlie)*, Luce Fabiole *(Julie's mother)*, Sylvine Delannoy *(Mme. Morane)*, Jacqueline Rouillard *(Maid)*, Van Doude *(Inspector Fabri)*, Paul Pavel *(Mechanic)*, Maurice Garell *(Plaintiff)*, Gilles Quéant *(Examining magistrate)*, Alexandra Stewart *(Mlle. Becker)*, Frédérique and Renaud Fontanarosa *(Musicians)*.

BAISERS VOLES (STOLEN KISSES). 1968. *Screenplay:* François Truffaut, Claude de Givray, Bernard Revon. *Photography* (Eastman Colour): Denys Clerval. *Art Director:* Claude Pignot.

*Editor:* Agnès Guillemot. *Music:* Antoine Duhamel. *Song* "Que reste-t-il de nos amours?" *composed and sung by:* Charles Trenet. *Sound:* René Levert. *Producer:* Marcel Berbert. *Production:* Les Films du Carrosse/Artistes Associés. 8,190 feet. 91 minutes.

*Players:* Jean-Pierre Léaud *(Antoine Doinel)*, Delphine Seyrig *(Fabienne Tabard)*, Claude Jade *(Christine Darbon)*, Michel Lonsdale *(M. Tabard)*, Harry Max *(M. Henri)*, André Falcon *(M. Blady)*, Claire Duhamel *(Mme. Darbon)*, Daniel Ceccaldi *(M. Darbon)*, Paul Pavel *(M. Julien)*, Serge Rousseau *(The man)*, Martine Ferrière *(Manageress of shoe shop)*, Catherine Lutz *(Mme. Catherine)*, Simono *(Conjurer's friend)*, Roger Trapp *(Hotel manager)*, Jacques Delord *(Conjurer)*, Jacques Rispal *(Deceived husband)*, Martine Brochard *(Unfaithful wife)*, Robert Cambourakis *(Lover)*, Marie-France Pisier *(Colette)*, Jean-François Adam *(Her husband)*.


LA SIRENE DU MISSISSIPI. 1969. *Screenplay:* François Truffaut. *Based on the novel* Waltz into Darkness *by:* William Irish. *Photography* (Eastman Colour/Dyaliscope): Denys Clerval. *Art Director:* Claude Pignot. *Editor:* Agnès Guillemot. *Music:* Antoine Duhamel. *Sound:* René Levert. *Producer:* Marcel Berbert. *Production:* Les Films du Carrosse/Artistes Associés/Produzioni Associate Delphos (Rome). 123 minutes.

*Players:* Jean-Paul Belmondo *(Louis Mahe)*, Catherine Deneuve *(Marion/Julie Roussel)*, Michel Bouquet *(Comolli)*, Nelly Borgeaud *(Berthe Roussel)*, Marcel Berbert *(Jardine)*, Martine Ferrière *(Landlady)*, Roland Thenot *(Richard)*.


*Opposite: Antoine in the shoe shop in BAISERS VOLES*

L'ENFANT SAUVAGE. 1970. *Screenplay:* François Truffaut, Jean Gruault. *Based on the book* Mémoire et Rapport sur Victor de l'Aveyron *by:* Jean Itard. *Photography:* Nestor Almendros. *Art Director:* Jean Mandroux. *Editor:* Agnès Guillemot. *Sound:* René Levert. *Producer:* Marcel Berbert. *Production:* Les Films du Carrosse/Artistes Associés.

*Players:* Jean-Pierre Cargol *(Victor, the "Beast Boy"),* Paul Ville *(Rémy),* François Truffaut *(Jean Itard),* Françoise Seigner *(Madame Guerin),* Claude Miler *(Monsieur Lemeri),* Annie Miler *(Madame Lemeri).*

Truffaut has written the scripts for the following films: *Tire au Flanc* (*dir.* Claude de Givray, 1961), *Une Grosse Tête* (*dir.* Claude de Givray, 1961), and *Mata-Hari* (*dir.* Jean-Louis Richard, 1964). He is usually credited with the (non-existent) script of Jean-Luc Godard's *A Bout de Souffle* (1959), to which he lent the prestige of his name, thus helping Godard raise the necessary finances.

Through his production company Les Films du Carrosse he has produced or co-produced the following: *Paris Nous Appartient* (*dir.* Jacques Rivette, 1960), *Le Testament d'Orphée* (*dir.* Jean Cocteau, 1960), *Tire au Flanc* (*dir.* Claude de Givray, 1961), *Mata-Hari* (*dir.* Jean-Louis Richard, 1964), *Deux ou Trois Choses que Je Sais d'Elle* (*dir.* Jean-Luc Godard, 1967), *L'Enfance Nue* (*dir.* Maurice Pialat, 1968), *Ma Nuit chez Maud* (*dir.* Eric Rohmer, 1969).

# Bibliography

A. *Scripts*
   1. Truffaut, François. *The 400 Blows.* New York: Grove Press, 1969. This includes some reviews and critical articles on the film.

2. Truffaut, François. *Jules and Jim*. London: Lorrimer; New York: Simon and Schuster, 1968.

3. Truffaut, François. *"La Peau Douce,"* *L'Avant-Scène Cinéma* (Paris), no. 48 (1965).

B. *Works by and about Truffaut*

4. Truffaut, François. *Hitchcock*. London: Secker & Warburg, 1968; New York: Simon and Schuster, 1967. Originally published as *Le Cinéma Selon Hitchcock*. Paris: Robert Laffont, 1966.

5. Truffaut, François. "Journal of *Fahrenheit 451*," *Cahiers du Cinéma in English* (New York), no. 5 (1967), 11-22; no. 6 (1967), 11-23; no. 7 (1967), 9-19. Translated from *Cahiers du Cinéma* (Paris), nos. 175-180 (February-July, 1966).

6. Bluestone, George. "The Fire and the Future," *Film Quarterly* (Berkeley), vol. 20, no. 4 (Summer, 1967), 3-10.

7. Comolli, Jean-Louis, and Narboni, Jean. "Interview with Truffaut," *Cahiers du Cinéma* (Paris), no. 190 (May, 1967), 20-30, 69-70.

8. [Ronder, Paul] (trans.). "François Truffaut—an Interview," *Film Quarterly* (Berkeley), vol. 17, no. 1 (Fall, 1963), 3-13. Translated and abridged from *Cahiers du Cinéma*, no. 138 (December, 1962).

9. Gramont, Sanche de. "Life Style of Homo Cinematicus— François Truffaut," *New York Times Magazine* (June 15, 1969), 12, 34-47.

10. Greenspun, Roger. "Elective Affinities: Aspects of *Jules and Jim*," *Sight and Sound* (London), vol. 32 (Spring, 1963), 78-82.

11. Marcorelles, Louis. "Interview with François Truffaut," *Sight and Sound* (London), vol. 31 (Winter, 1961-62), 35-37, 48.

12. Millar, Gavin. "Hitchcock versus Truffaut," *Sight and Sound* (London), vol. 38 (Spring, 1969), 82-88.

13. Rivette, Jacques. "Du Côté de chez Antoine," *Cahiers du Cinéma* (Paris), no. 95 (May, 1959), 37-39.
14. Shatnoff, Judith. "François Truffaut: The Anarchist Imagination," *Film Quarterly* (Berkeley), vol. 16, no. 3 (Spring, 1963), 3-11.

C. *Novels on which the Films are based*
15. Bradbury, Ray. *Fahrenheit 451.* London: Rupert Hart-Davis, 1954; New York: Ballantine Books, 1953.
16. Goodis, David. *Down There.* New York: Fawcett, 1956.
17. Irish, William (pseud. for Cornell George Hopley-Woolrich). *Waltz into Darkness.* New York: J. B. Lippincott, 1947.
18. Roché, Henri-Pierre. *Jules et Jim.* Paris: Gallimard, 1953. Translation by Patricia Evans. London: John Calder, 1963; New York: Hillary, 1953.
19. Woolrich, Cornell (pseud. for Hopley-Woolrich). *The Bride Wore Black.* New York: Simon and Schuster, 1940.

D. *Other Works referred to in the text*
20. Barthes, Roland. *Writing Degree Zero.* London: Jonathan Cape; New York: Hill and Wang, 1968.
21. Goffman, Erving. *The Presentation of Self in Everyday Life.* (rev. ed.) London: Allen Lane The Penguin Press, 1969; New York: Doubleday Anchor Books, 1959.
22. Hall, Edward T. *The Hidden Dimension.* New York: Doubleday, 1966.
23. ———. *The Silent Language.* New York: Doubleday, 1959.
24. Sontag, Susan. *Against Interpretation and Other Essays.* London: Eyre and Spottiswoode, 1966; New York: Farrar, Strauss, Giroux, 1966.
25. Wollen, Peter. *Signs and Meaning in the Cinema.* London: Secker & Warburg, 1969.